FASTING
with
GOD

TAMMY HOTSENPILLER

CHARISMA
HOUSE

FASTING WITH GOD by Tammy Hotsenpiller

Published by Charisma House, an imprint of Charisma Media

600 Rinehart Road, Lake Mary, Florida 32746

For more resources like this, visit charismahouse.com and the author's website at www.tammyhotsenpiller.com.

Cataloging-in-Publication Data is on file with the Library of Congress.

International Standard Book Number: 978-1-63641-271-9

E-book ISBN: 978-1-63641-272-6

23 24 25 26 27 — 9 8 7 6 5 4 3 2 1

Printed in the United States of America

Most Charisma Media products are available at special quantity discounts for bulk purchase for sales promotions, premiums, fund-raising, and educational needs. For details, call us at (407) 333-0600 or visit our website at www.charismamedia.com.

Tammy Hotsenpiller has written what I believe to be the most important book on the fasting subject in the twenty-first century.

Many authors have opened our eyes to the importance of fasting to achieve spiritual power and authority. However, to my knowledge, no one has taken on the task of combining the Hebrew names of God. This book is truly a seminal work that will expand both your heart and mind.

When the Disciples failed at the request to cast a demon, Jesus reminded them that "this kind (demon) does not go out except by prayer and fasting." (Matthew 17:21)

Prayer moves mountains, but prayer and fasting move spiritual forces aligned against us!

Tammy has been a consummate prayer warrior and spiritual leader in the area of fasting for breakthroughs that would have otherwise been impossible.

Our first twenty-one day church-wide fast enabled us to purchase our first building and set the tone for our church. I am so proud of my wife, who has authored eight books and helped lead our church to influence the world for Christ.

God wants you to experience new levels of spiritual power. This can be achieved only by prayer and fasting. I encourage you to use this resource as a tool to discover your true potential.

Phil Hotsenpiller
Influence Church, Senior Pastor
American Faith, President

ENDORSEMENTS

I have personally known Tammy for over ten years. Her heart for prayer and teaching the Word of God has been an ongoing inspiration to me.

Fasting with God is a powerful and supernatural workbook that will guide you through deeper intimacy with God.

Tammy has beautifully expounded upon the names and characteristics of God, along with daily fasting passages and assignments. This twenty-one day journey is sure to take you deeper in your understanding of God and the power of fasting.

Kristen Dalton Wolfe
Former Miss USA
Founder of Train To Reign Coaching

Tammy has a heart for women and prayer. This isn't just a book; it's a journey you are invited into with God. The names of God combined with Tammy's insight and Scripture are so powerful. What a blessing to our generation!

Lydia McLaughlin
TV Personality, Published Author, & Magazine Editor
Orange County, CA

When David encountered Goliath, he never called him a giant, nor did he call him a champion as the others did. David never even used Goliath's name. Instead, David called him a reproach and a defiler of the armies of Israel. David knew the power of a name, and because of this, David invoked courage and strength by calling on God with three of His many names. David called God "The Lord of Hosts," "The Living God," and most importantly "Jehovah." This final name that David invoked was the most significant. God's personal name, when combined with His manifold abilities, literally says of God, "I will be for you whatever you need when you need it." All this is to say, I cannot think of a more profound way to find strength in the physical weakness of fasting than to invoke and focus on the manifold strength of God as David did.

Tammy's book is so profound to employ exactly what David did to vanquish a tyrant like Goliath. The people of God will now be equipped to fast and pray in a manner that brings victory. The Holy Spirit has truly blessed us with the timeliness of this fasting and prayer blueprint to victory. Read it, apply it, and get ready to watch the giants begin to fall.

Rob McCoy
Senior Pastor, Calvary Chapel Godspeak
Former Mayor of Thousand Oaks, CA

We serve an eternal God who reveals Himself in innumerable ways through His Word. One of the amazing ways we come to know God more deeply is by discovering His names, which reveal His divine character. In Fasting with God, Tammy Hotsenpiller invites you on a journey to go deeper in your relationship with God, especially during a season of fasting and prayer.

This workbook is full of practical insights and biblical truth that will help take your focus from the realm of the visible to the realm of the Spirit.

The Word of God encourages us to pray with fasting, declaring that when we do, God will pour out His Spirit on all flesh. That is when we will see true transformation in our lives and in the world around us!

Dr. Ché Ahn
President, Harvest International Ministry
Senior Pastor,
Harvest Rock Church, Pasadena, CA
International Chancellor, Wagner University

Tammy takes us on an intimate journey with the Lord. One that is Biblically taught and spiritually and physically healing.

Thank you to Tammy for her heart for others in teaching the way to lean in to Jehovah like never before while offering up daily personal sacrifices.

David Scarlett
Radio Host, Pastor
His Glory Ministries, Valley City, OH

What a timely resource for the times we're living in! Part of every believer's walk with God is understanding who He is, and Fasting with God *uncovers not only the power behind God's name, but what that power means in our own lives. If you're looking for a resource to take you deeper in your faith and grow in your knowledge of God, this is it!*

Mike Kai
Pastor, Author, Influencer
Inspire Church, Honolulu, HI

Tammy's new book, Fasting with God, *is an amazing tool to help us understand fasting at a deeper level and to connect with God in a greater way.*

I love going through all the names of God and the way Tammy lays out each chapter with questions and prayer. If you would like to grow in your understanding of fasting and your relationship with God, check this book out!

Kim Walker-Smith
Founding Member of Jesus Culture,
Singer/Songwriter

I believe in the power of fasting and contending prayer to change our personal lives but also change the course of human history. Tammy's book provides us with insight, depth, and the theological understanding of why this is so crucial in our day.

Sean Feucht
Missionary, Artist, Speaker, Author, Activist
Founder of Hold The Line & Let Us Worship

Fasting might feel overwhelming, but this guide will help us not only understand but practice the beauty of fasting. I loved it!

Bianca Juarez Olthoff
Pastor, Author, Teacher
The Father's House OC, Anaheim, CA

Proverbs 18:10

The name of the Lord
is a strong tower;
The righteous run
to it and are safe.

Psalms 20:7

Some trust in chariots
and some in horses,
but we trust
in the name of the
LORD our God.

NAMES OF GOD

ABBA
Father

ADONAI
Lord

ALPHA & OMEGA
Beginning & End

CHRISTOS
The Anointed One

ELOHIM
The Creator

EL DEAH
God Of Knowledge

EL ELYON
The God Most High

EL MOSHAAH
God Of Salvation /
God The Deliverer

EL OLAM
The Everlasting God

EL SHADDAI
God Almighty

EL QANNA
Jealous God

HOLY SPIRIT
Helper / Comforter

JEHOVAH JIREH
The LORD Will Provide

JEHOVAH M'KADDESH
The Lord My Sanctifier

JEHOVAH NISSI
The LORD My Banner

JEHOVAH RA'AH
The Shepherd

JEHOVAH RAPHA
The LORD That Heals

JEHOVAH SABAOTH
The LORD Of Host

JEHOVAH SHALOM
The LORD Is Peace

JEHOVAH SHAMMAH
The LORD Is There

JEHOVAH TSIDKENU
The LORD Our
Righteousness

YAHWEH
LORD He Is / I AM

YESHUA
Savior / Jesus / Messiah

DAY 01

ELOHIM
The Creator

DAY 08

JEHOVAH RAPHA
The Lord That Heals

DAY 02

YAHWEH
LORD He Is / I Am

DAY 09

JEHOVAH NISSI
The Lord My Banner

DAY 03

EL ELYON
The God Most High

DAY 10

EL QANNA
Jealous God

DAY 04

ADONAI
Lord

DAY 11

JEHOVAH M'KADDESH
The Lord My Sanctifier

DAY 05

EL SHADDAI
God Almighty

DAY 12

JEHOVAH SHALOM
The LORD Is Peace

DAY 06

EL OLAM
The Everlasting God

DAY 13

JEHOVAH SABAOTH
The Lord of Host

DAY 07

JEHOVAH JIREH
The Lord Will Provide

DAY 14

EL DEAH
God Of Knowledge

TABLE OF CONTENTS

INTRODUCTION

name | nām |

noun

a word by which a person is known, addressed or referred to.

When you hear your name called out, it catches your attention. That's because our names represent who we are and a little bit about us. Most of us have several names that we go by. I know I do.

My husband calls me "Babe," my close friends call me "Tams," my children call me "Mom" or "Mother," my grandbabies call me "Gammy" and "Gigi," my mother called me "Tamara," "Darling," or "Sweetie," my sisters, well, they have called me a variety of names, some of which still haunt me today.

When our names are called out, we know them. We identify with them. We answer to them. God does as well. When we call out His name, He answers us.

The Name of God is all-powerful and eternal. We find a list of several names of God in the Bible. Jehovah/Yahweh (Lord), Elohim (Creator), Jesus, and Holy Spirit are all names that refer to God.

As you read the Bible, you will discover that God reveals Himself to us through His characteristics and attributes. He starts in Genesis with the name Elohim (Creator) and then continues to move through the pages to reveal Himself as Yahweh/Jehovah (Lord) and many more that we will discuss in this guide.

God continues to introduce Himself to humanity by additional names to assist them and meet them through struggle, difficulty, trial, or victory.

The names of God show us the many different ways He is present for us.

Do not take the Lord's name in vain.
Exodus 20:7

God takes His name seriously. That's because He knows all power and authority come through His name. There is no other name given by which we can be saved besides the name of Jesus.

Salvation is found in no one else, for there is no other name under heaven given to mankind by which we must be saved.
Acts 4:12

Fasting without the knowledge of who God is becomes just a ritual or routine. My desire for you is to understand and comprehend the personal names of God and the Power and Authority that come through His name.

And Jesus came and said to them, "All authority in Heaven and on earth has been given to me." Matthew 28:18

Fasting is giving up food or other things for a period of time to focus your thoughts and attention on God.

Often fasting is combined with prayer, and requests are made to God. In the Old Testament, fasting was common when times of grieving or repentance were necessary. In the New Testament, fasting is recommended as a way to grow in deeper communion with God. Similar to God's instructions on prayer, fasting is to be a personal decision and spiritual discipline.

In our time together on this fast, I want to lead you through the Names of God.

Each day we will research a new name, title, characteristic, behavior, or attribute of God.

I have found when I combine my prayer and my fast with the names of God, it's like praying with power. It's like a boost or spiritual charge because it reminds me of the capacity of my request and the faithfulness of God.

I did not grow up fasting. I know many religions and expressions of faith were taught to fast, especially during Holy Week, but that was not the case for me. I knew about fasting. I read about it in the Bible, and I was even taught the Scriptures in Sunday School, but it was not a personal practice. It wasn't until much later in life that I realized the expectation and direction that God gives us to practice fasting. Jesus Himself said some things only happen by prayer and fasting. (Matthew 17:21)

As we begin this study guide, I will show you the various types of fasting.

Through Scripture and personal examples, we will see why Jesus tells us to fast.

Then each day, we will look at a different name of God to combine our prayer, our fast, and our faith in God to see answers and breakthroughs in our personal lives.

At the time of this writing, I am preparing this study guide for our 10th Anniversary at Influence Church.

Our church began on February 12, 2012, and God truly has performed miracles and healings, along with writing great worship songs and living out the Word through so many ministries.

I wanted to provide our church with a resource guide to fast for twenty-one days before celebrating our 10th Anniversary.

But for those of you who have picked up this study guide for a different reason, I pray Holy Spirit would lead you, teach you, guide you, and empower you to see the deeper things of God by knowing His name.

WHAT TO EXPECT

When you fast, your body detoxifies and eliminates toxins from your system.

This can cause mild discomfort such as headaches and irritability during withdrawal from caffeine and sugars.

And naturally, you will have hunger pains and cravings.

Limit your activity, and exercise moderately. Take time to rest.

Fasting brings about miraculous results.

Remember, you are exercising a spiritual discipline when you fast.

Spend time listening to praise and worship music.

Pray as often as you can throughout the day.

Get away from the normal distractions as much as possible, and keep your heart and mind fixed on seeking God's face.

STEPS TO TAKE

STEPS TO TAKE BEFORE YOUR FAST

1. WHY ARE YOU FASTING?

Be specific. Why are you fasting? Do you need direction, healing, restoration in your marriage or a family matter? Are you facing financial difficulties? Are you joining a corporate fast?

2. GET PREPARED

Ask Holy Spirit to reveal areas of temptation and weakness. Forgive those who have offended you, and ask for forgiveness from those you may have offended. Surrender your life fully to Christ, and examine your heart for anything that might hinder you from all God has in store for you. (Romans 12:1-2)

3. DECIDE WHICH FAST IS RIGHT FOR YOU

The type of fasting you choose is up to you. You could go on an absolute fast in which you only drink liquids, or you may desire to fast like Daniel, who abstained from sweets and meats and drank only water. Remember to use the time you would normally eat to engage in prayer and Bible reading.

4. LONG FOR AN INTIMATE EXPERIENCE WITH GOD

I reach out for You. I thirst for You as parched land thirsts for rain. Psalm 143:6

The Psalmist had a deep longing to know the heart of God. Intimacy with God starts with a longing and then becomes a lifestyle.

Don't rush your devotion time with God. Make this experience a priority and a self-discovery of all that God has for your life.

DON'T RUSH YOUR DEVOTION TIME WITH GOD. MAKE THIS EXPERIENCE A PRIORITY AND A SELF-DISCOVERY OF ALL THAT GOD HAS FOR YOUR LIFE.

BENEFITS OF FASTING

1. HELPS US OVERCOME PERSONAL CHALLENGES

Fasting brings a sense of humility, as we must rely on God alone.
(Psalm 35:13; 69:10)

Esther fasted when faced with danger.
(Esther 4:16)

Ezra fasted for protection.
(Ezra 8:21-28)

Jehoshaphat fasted in the time of war.
(2 Chronicles 20:3)

Jesus fasted in the wilderness when confronted with the devil.
(Matthew 4:2)

2. OPENS OUR CONNECTION WITH GOD

Jesus said that His disciples would fast when He is gone.
(Mark 2:20)

When we fast, we open ourselves up to a renewed presence of God.

3. EMPOWERS US TO WALK IN THE SPIRIT AND LIVE OUT OUR TESTIMONY

In the Old Testament, we often see people fasting in a time of crisis; in the New Testament, we see Jesus fasted for His calling. We should fast during problems and as a testimony of God's power and sufficiency in our lives. Anna fasted as she stood at the gate, waiting to see the Messiah.
(Luke 2:37)

4. DEFEATS THE DEVIL

When the disciples of Jesus could not cast out a demon, Jesus said, "This kind does not leave, but by prayer and fasting."
(Matthew 17:21)

Fasting helps break the bonds of wickedness, undo heavy burdens, and empower us to break every yoke.
(Isaiah 58:6)

FASTING HELPS
BREAK THE
BONDS OF
WICKEDNESS,
UNDO HEAVY
BURDENS, AND
EMPOWER US
TO BREAK
EVERY YOKE

TYPE OF FAST

We all fast, whether we realize it or not. God created us to fast. Let's say you sleep seven to eight hours a night. That is fasting. No food intake for several hours. That is why we will call our first meal of the day "breakfast," because we break our fast.

When Jesus was speaking to the crowd in Matthew 6:16, He said, "When you fast" (not IF you fast).

So fasting is to be part of our lives. A personal discipline and action that we engage in with God. We are a tripart being. Body-Soul-Spirit. Just as our bodies long for physical food, our spirits long for spiritual food.

The act of fasting forces our spirits to rely on God to feed us.

In John 4:32, the disciples were concerned because Jesus had not yet eaten.

"But He said to them, 'I have food to eat that you know nothing about.' " Jesus was teaching them the truth about fasting and the Word of God.

Fasting makes us dependent on the resources of God.

It causes us to believe God will meet our needs and increase our faith and trust in Him.

There are a few different types of fasts you can do.

ABSOLUTE FAST / FULL FAST / COMPLETE FAST

This can either be fasting from food and drink or only drinking liquids (you establish the number of days).

This is not for everyone. It is a very intense and potentially dangerous type of fast. The Bible is clear to say that God led them and sustained them.

Make sure you check with your physician before starting an absolute fast.

Moses and Jesus fasted for forty days, but let me remind you that this was a supernatural or miraculous fast.

JESUS

"Jesus, full of the Holy Spirit, left the Jordan and was led by the Spirit into the wilderness, where for forty days he was tempted by the devil. He ate nothing during those days, and at the end of them, he was hungry." Luke 4:1-2

MOSES

"When I was gone up into the mount to receive the tables of stone, even the tables of the covenant which the LORD made with you, then I abode in the mount forty days, and forty nights, I neither did eat bread nor drink water." Deuteronomy 9:9

PARTIAL FAST

In a partial fast, you choose certain hours to abstain from food. Say, sunup to sundown. Or nothing to eat until noon. The times are up to you.

"When I heard these things, I sat down and wept. For some days I mourned and fasted and prayed before the God of heaven." Nehemiah 1:4

JUICE / LIQUID FAST

Fruit and vegetable juices only. You only drink liquids for twenty-one days. Juice, shakes, coffee, water, etc.

"...and then was a widow until she was eighty-four. She never left the temple but worshiped night and day, fasting and praying." Luke 2:37

THE DANIEL FAST

You don't eat any meat or sweets or bread. Drink water and juice. You eat only fruits and vegetables.

"Please test your servants for ten days: Give us nothing but vegetables to eat and water to drink." Daniel 1:12

"So I turned to the Lord God and pleaded with him in prayer and petition, in fasting, and in sackcloth and ashes." Daniel 9:3

"I ate no choice food; no meat or wine touched my lips; and I used no lotions at all until the three weeks were over." Daniel 10:3

OTHER FAST / ABSTINENCE

Fast from a personal pleasure: social media, television, alcohol, shopping, etc. These are all good areas to have self-discipline. Your fast is personal and should be something God speaks to you about and leads you to do. You abstain from something God has led you to give up.

For those with a medical condition, you may want to choose this type of fast.

In the Bible, we see several examples of other fasts.

SOME EXAMPLES:
• Oils - Daniel 10:3
• Physical relationships - 1 Corinthians 7:5;
   Exodus 19:15
• Certain things such as foods, people, places,
   practices - Joshua 3:5

CORPORATE FAST / GROUP FAST

Join a group of believers to fast and pray for a specific matter.

This is the type of fast we are doing as a church.

We are asking God to do a new work and bring a fresh move of His Spirit. We have been invited to participate in a group fast with a specific outcome.

Esther appealed to God's people to come together in a corporate fast for the welfare of the Jews.

"Go, gather together all the Jews who are in Susa, and fast for me. Do not eat or drink for three days, night or day. I and my attendants will fast as you do. When this is done, I will go to the king, even though it is against the law. And if I perish, I perish." Esther 4:16

ISOLATION / SEPARATION FAST

While Jesus did not give us a detailed outline of things we are to abstain from during a fast, He did model isolation as a means to truly focus on God. Jesus often withdrew from His disciples to spend time alone with God.

"But Jesus often withdrew to lonely places and prayed." Luke 5:16

Fasting makes us dependent on the resources of God.

HOW IT WORKS

Each day you will work through a process of studying the names of God, a fasting passage, your daily assignment, your prayer time, and then any journal entry you may want to record.

I believe this will be one of the greatest experiences you have had in your spiritual journey. Prayer and fasting are keys to breakthrough and power.

DAILY ASSIGNMENT

Read the description of the Name of God, along with the correlating fasting passage. Take time to work through your daily assignment. The questions are a combination of the Name of God and the fasting passage studied that day.

DAILY CLOSING PRAYER

Prayer is the most powerful form of communication we have access to. Greater than our phones, or social media, or our personal conversations. Prayer is talking to God. After each assignment, you will end with a prayer. Take time to read the prayer and make it your own.

JOURNAL ENTRY

Over the next twenty-one days, you will discover new things about God and His many characteristics, but you will also discover new things about yourself. At the end of each day, there will be a place for you to journal your thoughts and self-discovery. Use this opportunity to write down your journey and the many things God is showing you.

ADDITIONAL THOUGHTS

If you need additional space to journal your thoughts, please see the back of the guide.

DISCLAIMER

Please check with your physician before beginning any fast or change in diet routine.

THE
JOURNEY

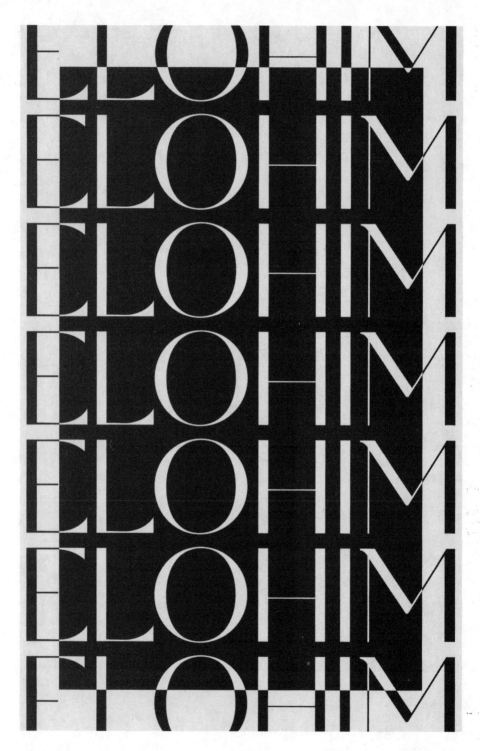

48

Elohim (Creator)

Elohim is the primary name used for God in the Old Testament and is used 2,599 times throughout the Bible to refer to God as Mighty, Powerful, and the Creator over all.

Elohim is the first name given to God and is found in the very first verse of Genesis 1:1.

"In the beginning God (Elohim) created the heavens and the earth." Genesis 1:1

The term "Elohim" means "supreme one" or "mighty one." He is the great and powerful God that shows His authority by His creation.

"For the Lord your God (Elohim) is God of gods and Lord of lords, the great God, mighty and awesome, who shows no partiality and accepts no bribes." Deuteronomy 10:17

Elohim is the infinite, all-powerful God

ELOHIM

who shows by His works that He is the Creator, Sustainer, and Supreme Judge of the world.

"El" means "God," as we will see in several of the names we study together. El Elyon - "The Most High God," El Shaddai - "God Almighty," El Qanna - "Jealous God," El Olam - "The Everlasting God"... As you can see, each name refers to God, along with one of His many attributes. More to come on this.

The *him* - ending of Elohim - is very important because it is a plural ending and is believed to be a reference to the Trinity, which we will see again in Genesis 1:26 when we read, "Let Us make man in our own image."

In Mark 15:34, when Jesus cried out from the cross, *"Eloi, Eloi, lema sabachthani?"* He was calling the Father with a form of *Elohim, Eloi.* "My God, my God, why have You forsaken me?"

We also see *Elohim* defined as Great and Powerful. His glory is witnessed in the things He has made.

"Ah, Sovereign LORD, you have made the heavens and the earth by your great power and

outstretched arm. Nothing is too hard for you."
Jeremiah 32:17

This great power is the characteristic of God known by His name Elohim.

As we see from today's study, our *Elohim* is mighty and strong and the Creator of all things. Including you. God saw you before you were born. He knew the gifts and abilities He wired you with.

The destiny and opportunities He laid out for your future, for He is our Creator God.

Take some time today and focus on all the creativity God has given you. Elohim is the Creator God, and He has made us in His image. We have the ability to create ideas, concepts, music, poems, books, and brands.

God loves to see His children productive and creative when it is done for His glory and good.

FAST FOR A RIGHT MOTIVE

Matthew 6:16-18

"When you fast, do not look somber as the hypocrites do, for they disfigure their faces to show others they are fasting. Truly I tell you, they have received their reward in full. But when you fast, put oil on your head and wash your face, so that it will not be obvious to others that you are fasting, but only to your Father, who is unseen; and your Father, who sees what is done in secret, will reward you."

Jesus made a point to teach His disciples and followers about fasting.

Many in that day were using the act of fasting to look spiritual, righteous, and holy.

Jesus said...stop it.

When you fast, make it private and an act of intimacy and connection.

Our Father knows our hearts and motives.

Don't announce you are fasting to get others to think you are Godly or pious.

Wash your face (don't look like you're starving, lol), get dressed as you would any day, and make your fast a gift, and worship unto God.

Read the entire chapter of Matthew 6.

Begin your fast with the right attitude and heart motive.

Fasting is an act of worship and discipline.

It is not for show or spirituality.

Be cautious not to use your fast as a demonstration of your righteousness.

Ask God to show you things in your life that need to be surrendered and confessed.

A clean heart and pure motive are the only way to begin your twenty-one-day fast.

1. What do you need to surrender or confess to God?

_____

_____

_____

_____

2. What stood out to you when reading Matthew Chapter 6?

_____

_____

_____

_____

3. What is something you are asking God to do through this fast? Ask Elohim, the Supreme One, the Mighty One, to empower you with His strength and goodness.

_____

_____

_____

_____

WHENEVER I
THINK OF THE
WORD "INTIMACY,"
I THINK OF IN-TO-ME-SEE.
ASK GOD TO SHOW YOU
WHAT GREAT LOVE HE HAS
FOR YOU TODAY.

"

Prayer is when you talk to
God; meditation is when you
listen to God.

Anonymous

DEAR ELOHIM,

I ask for Your guidance and protection over me today as I begin this fast.

I ask You to show me Your creative beauty and goodness in all I see today.

I pray as I grow in my intimacy with You that I begin to understand Your great love for me.

Give me Wisdom as I go about my day.

In Jesus' Name,
Amen

Journal Entry

_____

_____

_____

_____

_____

_____

DAILY PRAYER

YAHWEH

YAHWEH

YAHWEH

Yahweh (LORD, Jehovah / He is / I AM)

Yahweh is one of the most used names for God and is found 6,519 times in the Bible. We first see Yahweh appear in Genesis 2:4.

"This is the account of the heavens and the earth when they were created, when the LORD God (Yahweh) made the earth and the heavens."
Genesis 2:4

It speaks of His Eternal Presence.

Yahweh is the promised proper name of God. It means *Self-existence*. By Jewish tradition, this name is too holy to pronounce or write. Therefore they just wrote four letters without any vowels: YHWH. Jews stopped saying the name altogether in the third century because they feared violating the fourth commandment, which prohibits misusing or taking the Lord's name in vain.

Therefore, scholars today don't know for sure if the original pronunciation was

YAHWEH

Yahweh or Jehovah.

Whenever YHWH occurs as a compound name with other words, it is translated Jehovah instead.

Much of the opinion today is that "Yahweh" is the original pronunciation and that the meaning is "He Is" or "I AM." When God spoke to Moses at the burning bush, He introduced Himself as the Great I AM. Moses asked, "Who shall I say sent me?" God replied, "Tell them (Yahweh) the Great I AM sent you."

God said to Moses, "I AM WHO I AM. This is what you are to say to the Israelites: 'I AM has sent me to you.' "
Exodus 3:14

Jesus upset his generation, especially when He said, "Before Abraham was, I AM," in John 8:58.

"Very truly I tell you," Jesus answered, "before Abraham was born, I AM!"

He also claimed to be (Yahweh) in such phrases as "I AM the Light of the World," "the Bread of Life," "Living Water," "the Resurrection and the

Life," "The Way, the Truth and the Life," all found in the Gospel of John. When Jesus spoke again to the people, He said, "I am (Yahweh) the light of the world. Whoever follows me will never walk in darkness but will have the light of life." John 8:12

Jesus answered, "I am (Yahweh) the way and the truth and the life. No one comes to the Father except through me." John 14:6

Yahweh can also be seen as Jehovah or LORD (all capital letters). He is the One who is Self-existing, and He has permanent existence. He is the Great I AM.

FASTING FOR RIGHTEOUSNESS AND POWER

Isaiah 58

Once again, we see the people use fasting to impress God.

They play the role of God's children but have no power or mercy to show for their actions.

Read with me Isaiah 58:3b-4, 6-9:

"Yet on the day of your fasting, you do as you please and exploit all your workers. Your fasting ends in quarreling and strife, and in striking each other with wicked fists. You cannot fast as you do today and expect your voice to be heard on high."

God says enough... He reminds them of the reason for fasting in the first place. Continue to read with me. "Is not this the kind of fasting I have chosen: to loose the chains of injustice and untie the cords of the yoke, to set the oppressed free and break every yoke? Is it not to share your food with the hungry and to provide the poor wanderer with shelter—when you see the naked, to clothe them, and not to turn away from your own flesh and blood?

Then your light will break forth like the dawn, and your healing will quickly appear; then your righteousness will go before you, and the glory of the Lord will be your rear guard. Then you will call, and the Lord will answer, you will cry for help, and he will say: Here am I."

God wants our fasting to be filled with power and grace. He wants us to think of the welfare of others and the healing of all. We must all come to a place of surrender and humility toward others.

God's fast is different from that of the world. Yahweh is our Lord and Master, and apart from Him, we can do nothing. He is the Great I AM.

He is your everything. If you have a need or a struggle today, allow the Great I AM to fill your heart. What do you need?

He is the Great I AM.

Read the entire chapter of Isaiah 58.

As you have seen from the reading in Isaiah, the children of God seek God's attention and approval. They call out and ask Him why He does not answer, why He does not hear their plea. And God answers, "Don't you see your anger, your quarreling, your strife?"

"You cannot fast as you do today and expect your voice to be heard on high." Isaiah 58:4b

God in His goodness reminds the people what kind of fast is required for power and answered prayer. Stop for a minute and assess your last seven days. Have you loosened the chains of injustice or untied the cords of those in bondage? Have you done anything to set the oppressed free? Have you helped or encouraged others?

"What does this have to do with fasting?" you may be asking yourself. The truth is, when we fast, we make way for God to move, act, and use us for His service.

1. What is something you can do today to help someone in need?

_____

_____

_____

_____

2. Is there someone you need to ask forgiveness of or apologize to for your actions?

_____

_____

_____

_____

3. Where do you need to trust that The Great I AM is working on your behalf?

_____

_____

_____

_____

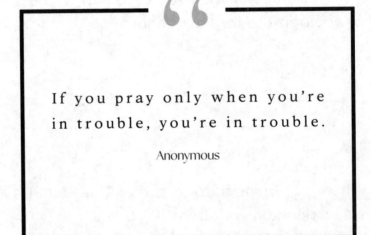

If you pray only when you're in trouble, you're in trouble.

Anonymous

DAILY PRAYER

DEAR YAHWEH (JEHOVAH),

Your Eternal Presence is felt in our world every day. I trust and know that You are The Great I AM and have already met my need and answered my prayer.

Thank You for Eternal Life and the joy I have in being a child of God.

As I fast today, I ask your Spirit to lead and guide me to those in need.

In Jesus' Name,
Amen

Journal Entry

_____

_____

_____

_____

_____

_____

EL ELYON

EL ELYON

EL ELYON

EL ELYON

EL ELYON

EL ELYON

El Elyon (The Most High God)

It is used fifty-two times in the Bible (sometimes without El, simply as Elyon).

El Elyon is first seen in Genesis 14:18.

"And Melchizedek king of Salem brought out bread and wine; now he was the priest of the God Most High (El Elyon)." Genesis 14:18

"El" is similar to the name Elohim and is used to speak of God. "Elyon" means most high or highest.

When combined with El, it means *The Most High God.*

It refers to the characteristic of God that is above everyone and everything.

This name describes His authority as the Sovereign and Holy God.

He is the God above all gods.

Our world is filled with opportunity and

EL ELYON

technology that emboldens us to believe we are more powerful than we are. It is easy to think we don't need God.

Between our busy schedules and endless opportunities, God gets relegated to a back shelf to be called on when needed.

But the truth is, He is God - the Most High God. And His ways are sovereign and beyond our understanding.

Satan thought he could go head-to-head with God, but look where he landed.

Isaiah 14:12-15:
"How you are fallen from heaven, O Lucifer, son of the morning! How you are cut down to the ground, you who weakened the nations! For you have said in your heart: 'I will ascend into heaven, I will exalt my throne above the stars of God; I will also sit on the mount of the congregation. On the farthest sides of the north; I will ascend above the heights of the clouds, I will be like the **Most High (El Elyon)**.' Yet you shall be brought down to Sheol, to the lowest depths of the Pit."

As humanity, we were created in the image of God, but that does not make us gods.

There is only One True God, One Eternal God, One God that is Most High, and His name is El Elyon.

Take a moment now and thank God for His watchcare and protection over your life.

FASTING FOR A PURE HEART

A Call to Repentance

Joel 2:12-16:

" 'Now, therefore,' says the Lord, 'turn to Me with all your heart, with fasting, with weeping, and with mourning. So rend your heart, and not your garments; return to the Lord your God, for He is gracious and merciful, slow to anger, and of great kindness; and He relents from doing harm. Who knows if He will turn and relent, and leave a blessing behind Him—a grain offering and a drink offering for the Lord your God? Blow the trumpet in Zion, consecrate a fast, call a sacred assembly; gather the people, sanctify the congregation, assemble the elders, gather the children and nursing babes; let the bridegroom go out from his chamber, and the bride from her dressing room.' "

The Lord is asking us to examine our hearts through repentance, fasting, weeping, and mourning.

The things that break the heart of God should break the hearts of His children. He uses the word "turn" to remind us we have a choice in what we do and how we behave.

Fasting is an act of our will and purifies our motives. In this passage, we see the call for a corporate fast.

A cry for families, individuals, and congregations to enter into a unified time of seeking God and repenting of any wrongdoing.

Meditate on today's passage: Joel 2:12-16.

In this passage, we see a call to repentance.

Repentance means to turn around and go the other way.

It is an act of our will and a conscience decision to go in a new direction.

Fasting brings about a purification of our hearts and a stirring in our souls to become one with God.

1. What is God showing you about this passage?

_____

_____

_____

_____

2. We don't talk about weeping and mourning much today, but for Israel it was a part of their culture. They understood the brokenness that comes from repentance.

What grieves your spirit? What breaks your heart? What are the things you see today that you know God is grieved about?

_____

_____

_____

_____

3. In this passage, we see a call for a corporate fast. Invite someone to join you on your fast. What are you fasting for today?

_____

_____

_____

_____

> "

Prayer should be the key of the
day and the lock of the night.

George Herbert

DEAR EL ELYON,

You are the Most High God. Your Presence is Eternal and Sovereign above all. Today I submit to Your will and Your call on my life.

I ask You to empower me with strength and confidence to be all You have created me to be.

I will not put any other gods before You, the King of Kings.

In Jesus' Name,
Amen

Journal Entry

_____
_____
_____
_____
_____
_____

DAILY PRAYER

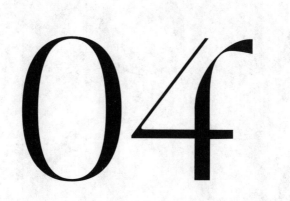

Adonai (Lord, Master)

It is used 434 times in the Bible.
We first see Adonai in Genesis 15:2.

"But Abram said, 'Lord GOD, what
will You give me seeing I go childless,
and the heir of my house is Eliezer of
Damascus?' "
Genesis 15:2

Abram understood the power and
authority of the One and Only True Lord.
Here we have a beautiful passage where
Abram understood his inability to have
children, and God took him outside to
count the stars in the sky. *See Abram,
you cannot count them all. So shall all
your descendants be. I will make you a
father of a great nation (Genesis 15:5).*

Abram understood Lordship, and the
Bible said it was credited to him as
righteousness.

According to Jewish tradition, you do
not speak or spell the name of God
(Yahweh).

ADONAI

As another option, they often would use Adonai instead of YHWH. Adonai means *Lord, Master,* or *Owner.*

This name confirmed that God leads and rules His creation and His people; He is Lord of lords.

Adonai translated "Lord" stresses His absolute authority.

1. The singular noun Adon means lord (over subjects) or master (over servants), which stresses His absolute authority.

2. The plural ending (-ai) attached to Adon marks Him as "Lord par excellence" or "Lord of all"—Psalm 136:3.

3. Adonai denotes God as the One who justifiably expects our honor and obedience. Joshua 5:13–15; Isaiah 6:1–8

Many of us call Jesus our Lord.

It is a word that has become common and comfortable to Christians. But the fact is that He is not really Lord to everyone.

"Not everyone who says to Me, 'Lord, Lord,' shall enter the kingdom of heaven, but he who does the will of My Father in heaven."
Matthew 7:21

This verse always bothered me because I can't imagine God not allowing those who love Him to enter Heaven. But notice the end of the verse: "but he who does the will of My Father in heaven." It is not enough to just call Him Lord.

You must make Him *your* Lord. When you put your trust and faith in Jesus, it was because He was the only One that could save you. It was because you said, *"You are my Lord."*

Have you taken Jesus off the throne of your life?

Today is the perfect day to re-crown Him *Lord of lords.*

OBEDIENCE BRINGS BLESSING

Jonah 3:1-5:

"Now the word of the Lord came to Jonah the second time, saying, 'Arise, go to Nineveh, that great city, and preach to it the message that I tell you.' So Jonah arose and went to Nineveh, according to the word of the Lord. Now Nineveh was an exceedingly great city, a three-day journey *in extent.* And Jonah began to enter the city on the first day's walk. Then he cried out and said, 'Yet forty days, and Nineveh shall be overthrown!' So the people of Nineveh believed God, proclaimed a fast, and put on sackcloth, from the greatest to the least of them."

Have you ever been prejudiced against someone? Most of us have. Jonah hated the Ninevites. He thought he was better and definitely godlier.

That's why he was the one chosen for the job. God had some work to do in Jonah.

Deep down, I think he hoped they would not repent and follow God.

But when the Spirit of the Lord is prompting you, you know you must follow.

Something happened to the Ninevites during the fast.

Their sin was exposed, and their hearts were open.

Fasting has a way of showing us our true selves.

Because of their repentance, God heard their cry and relented and didn't destroy their land.

Obedience brings blessing.

Read the entire chapter of Jonah 3.

1. How has your fast caused you to reevaluate your life?

_____

_____

_____

_____

2. What did you learn about the name Adonai that was new to you?

_____

_____

_____

_____

3. Is there an area in your life that you need to make Jesus Lord over again? How can you do that?

_____

_____

_____

_____

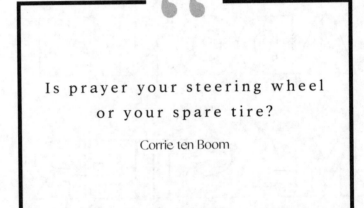

Is prayer your steering wheel
or your spare tire?

Corrie ten Boom

DEAR ADONAI,

You alone are Lord. Not my family, nor my job, nor my possessions.

I submit to You today and ask that You retake the throne of my life. Teach me to yield my all to You on an everyday basis.

Thank You for loving me and leading me in Your path of righteousness.

In Jesus' Name,
Amen

Journal Entry

_____

_____

_____

_____

_____

_____

DAILY PRAYER

05

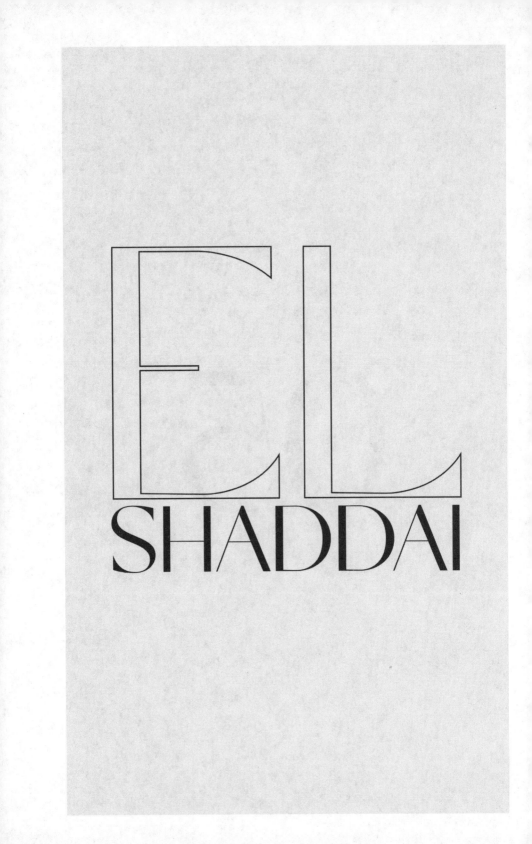

EL SHADDAI

El Shaddai (Lord God Almighty)

Used forty-eight times in the Bible (sometimes without El, simply as Shaddai).

First seen in Genesis 17:1-8:

"When Abram was ninety-nine years old, the Lord appeared to Abram and said to him, 'I *am* Almighty God (El Shaddai); walk before Me and be blameless. And I will make My covenant between Me and you, and will multiply you exceedingly.' Then Abram fell on his face, and God talked with him, saying: 'As for Me, behold, My covenant is with you, and you shall be a father of many nations. No longer shall your name be called Abram, but your name shall be Abraham; for I have made you a father of many nations. I will make you exceedingly fruitful; and I will make nations of you, and kings shall come from you. And I will establish My covenant between Me and you and your descendants after you in their generations, for an everlasting covenant, to be God to you and your descendants after you. Also I give to you and your descendants after you the land in which you are a stranger, all the land of Canaan, as an everlasting possession; and I will be their God.' "

Again, El is similar to the name Elohim and is used to speak of God.

Shaddai comes from the word for a woman's breast *(shad)* and literally means "many-breasted one." This denotes God as the provider, supplying, nourishing, and satisfying His people's needs as a mother would her child.

God Our Sustainer.

Shaddai is also related to the Hebrew word *shadad,* which means to overpower or destroy, referring to God's absolute power.

This describes God as the One who triumphs over every obstacle and all opposition.

Used together, El Shaddai is usually translated *Lord God Almighty.*

God is our all-powerful and all-sufficient sustainer.

If anyone needed to know God as their El Shaddai, it was Abram. With them being childless, God knew the desire of both Sarah and Abram and promised them a child from their own bodies. Yet, it would be their faith in an all-knowing and loving God that would activate the promise.

El Shaddai was the only one that could provide their request. *He was their provider.*

The book of Job uses the name *El Shaddai* more than any book in the Bible. God gives Job a particularly clear and awe-inspiring description and display of His power in Job 38-42.

FASTING FOR FREEDOM

Judges 20:26:

"Then all the children of Israel, that is, all the people, went up and came to the house of God and wept. They sat there before the Lord and fasted that day until evening; and they offered burnt offerings and peace offerings before the Lord."

Israel was at war with the tribe of Benjamin. The battles were fierce and bloody. Benjamin was a mighty and strong tribe that had won the conflict time and time again.

Fear and intimidation flooded the hearts of the Israelites, and they needed God to speak from Heaven.

Why is it we wait until the battles seem insurmountable before we seek the Lord in prayer and fasting?

This was the case with Israel. They were broken and beaten and now needed God to come through.

In repentance and weeping, Israel brought an offering unto the Lord.

God heard their cry and gave them step-by-step instructions to win the battle with the Benjamites.

The greatest freedom we experience is when we walk in faith and obedience with God.

Read Judges 20:26-46.

1. This battle was fierce. The enemy had won the past two battles, and now the people knew they had to turn to God for help. Sometimes it is hard to understand the ways of God.

But when His children cry out to Him with fasting and faith, He acts. (v. 26)

What battle are you fighting right now?

_____

_____

_____

_____

2. Your faith, along with your fast, move the heart of God. What steps and action can you take to turn your battle over to God today?

_____

_____

_____

_____

3. Breakthrough brings freedom. When we fast, we break the bondage of our past failures and defeats. Begin today to pray life and power over your setback and battles.

In the space provided below, write out your faith declaration of victory over your circumstances.

_____

_____

_____

_____

_____

_____

_____

_____

_____

_____

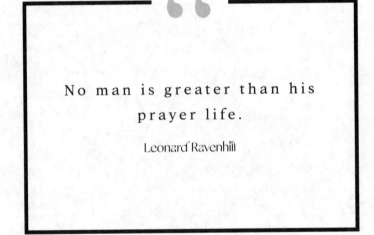

No man is greater than his
prayer life.

Leonard Ravenhill

DAILY PRAYER

DEAR EL SHADDAI,

You are my provider God, supplying, nourishing, and satisfying my needs.

I thank You for Your everlasting love and provision in my life.

I ask that You fight my battles and lead me in victory, confidence and freedom.

I yield to Your plans and path for my life today, as my El Shaddai.

In Jesus' Name,
Amen

Journal Entry

_____

_____

_____

_____

_____

EL OLAM

El Olam
(The Eternal and Everlasting God)

Used 439 times in the Bible.

First seen in Genesis 21:33.

"Abraham planted a tamarisk tree in
Beersheba, and there he called on the
name of the LORD, the Eternal God
(El Olam)."
Genesis 21:33

The definition of eternal is "lasting
or existing forever; without end or
beginning."

The journey into a deeper relationship
with God was ongoing for Abraham.

El Olam was the eternal and everlasting
God daily walking with him.

The story in this passage shows two
men in a disagreement, yet God gave
Abraham wisdom to discern the
moment.

A covenant was made between the two, and Abraham planted a tree as a memorial to the Eternal God - El Olam - as a tribute to His power.

El Olam is also found in another passage, Exodus 20:7, where the Bible says: "You shall not take the name of the LORD Your God in vain, for the LORD will not hold him guiltless who takes His name in vain."

This name for God refers to His Self-existence or His eternity.

God has always existed.

In today's culture, we have tried to make God's name common by using it as a figure of speech.

But this passage truly reveals the heart of God in the matter.

God's name is to be revered and respected.

Do not take the Lord's name in vain.

THE ETERNAL AND EVERLASTING GOD

FASTING FOR REVELATION

Luke 2:36-38:

"Now there was one, Anna, a prophetess, the daughter of Phanuel, of the tribe of Asher. She was of a great age and had lived with a husband seven years from her virginity; and this woman *was* a widow of about eighty-four years, who did not depart from the temple, but served *God* with fasting and prayers night and day. And coming in that instant she gave thanks to the Lord and spoke of Him to all those who looked for redemption in Jerusalem."

I love this passage. It is one of my favorites. Because this woman (Anna) did not give up.

She did not give in.

She fasted and believed in her prayer request.

That she would see in her lifetime the

Messiah, the Anointed One.

Her prayer was answered.

It just so happened that Mary and Joseph came
to the temple at the very moment she was
there.

How perfectly timely is our God?

Her fast fueled her faith!

Read Luke 2:36-38 again.

Do you think you would stand at the temple gate day after day waiting to see the Messiah?

Is your faith bold enough to withstand the long hours and endless disappointments that come along?

For Anna, she had hope and confidence that God would come through for her.

And He did.

1. How badly do you want to see Jesus?

Write a sentence to Him now asking for your prayer request.

_____

_____

_____

_____

2. What are the things that get in your way of waiting on Jesus to answer?
(impatience, disappointment, time, family, etc.?)

_____

_____

_____

_____

3. Today we are fasting for revelation.

Take a moment now and ask God to give you His wisdom, insight, and revelation for your future.

What did He show you today?

_____

_____

_____

_____

> ❝
>
> While a fast, by nature, is inconvenient, it should be an inconvenience to you—not to those around you.
>
> David Peach

DAILY PRAYER

DEAR EL OLAM,

You are the Eternal and Everlasting God.

You alone have wisdom and knowledge.

I ask that You fill me with Your Spirit and show me the steps to take today.

Teach me to look for Your divine revelation and to act with wisdom in my daily choices.

In Jesus' Name,
Amen

Journal Entry

_____
_____
_____
_____
_____
_____

JEHOVAH
JIREH

JEHOVAH JIREH

Jehovah Jireh (The Lord Will Provide)

Jehovah Jireh only occurs once in Genesis 22:14.

Genesis 22:11-14:

"But the Angel of the Lord called to Him from heaven and said, 'Abraham, Abraham!' So he said, 'Here I am.' And He said, 'Do not lay your hand on the lad, or do anything to him; for now I know that you fear God, since you have not withheld your son, your only *son*, from Me.' Then Abraham lifted his eyes and looked, and there behind *him* was a ram caught in a thicket by its horns. So Abraham went and took the ram, and offered it up for a burnt offering instead of his son. And Abraham called the name of the place, The-Lord-Will-Provide (Jehovah Jireh); as it is said *to* this day, 'In the Mount of the Lord it shall be provided.' "

Jehovah is translated as "The Existing One" or "Lord." The chief meaning of Jehovah is derived from the Hebrew

word Havah, meaning "to be" or "to exist."
It also suggests "to become" or specifically
"to become known" – this denotes a God who
reveals Himself to be known.

Jireh means Provider. Our Provider.

I think we all believe God will provide for our
well-being, but His timing is often questionable.
In this passage, we see that Abraham was
getting ready to see another dimension of God's
character. Jehovah Jireh. His provider. God had
called Abraham to go to Mt. Moriah and offer
his only son as a sacrifice.

Abraham knew God had given him this miracle
boy as a promise, but now his faith was being
tested by none other than God Himself. As
Abraham and Isaac made their way to the
mountain, I am sure Abraham prayed like never
before. If God gave me this son, then he is His to
do as He wills.

In obedience, Abraham took the wood and laid
it upon his son as a sacrifice unto God (a type
of wood similar to the wooden cross that Jesus
was placed upon as our sacrifice). He then
lifted his hand with the knife to sacrifice his son.

Then God spoke out and cried, "ABRAHAM, do not lay your hand on the boy, for now, I know you fear God. I am Jehovah Jireh... I AM YOUR PROVIDER."

God's timing is right on time. Even when we are in doubt, God is moving on our behalf. Is there something you need to offer God today that is standing in your way of seeing Him move?

We all need a Mt. Moriah experience where we are willing to be obedient to what God calls us to release unto Him. Stop right now and ask God to show you what you need to surrender to Him. What is your Isaac?

The word for provide, "Jireh," in the Old Testament is actually to *see*. When God sees, He foresees. He is omniscient, all-knowing, all-seeing, Eternal God. Earlier in the passage, Isaac looks to his father and says, "The fire and the wood are here, but where is the sacrifice?" Abraham replies, "God himself will PROVIDE the lamb for the burnt offering." Abraham knew God foresaw the moment as though it were the present moment. That is faith.

God is our Jehovah Jireh. Our Provider.

FASTING FOR PROVISION

Psalm 35:12-13:

"They reward me evil for good to the sorrow of my soul. But as for me, when they (David's enemies) were sick, My clothing *was* sackcloth; I humbled myself with fasting; and my prayer would return to my own heart."

David is in a dark and despairing place. His enemy is all around him, and he cries out to God for help.

This may have been the time in history when David was being pursued by King Saul. David calls to God for vindication and protection. "God, I have walked in Your ways," he reasons, "now where are You?"

Like David, many of us ask God, "Where are You?" The beauty of this passage and so many in the Bible is the journey to see God and connect with God.

David knows God has not left his side, and even though he feels overwhelmed by his circumstance, he knows God will see him through.

By the end of the Psalm, David is once again praising God. But the question is, what do we do in the in-between times?

The hard and lonely times?

The seasons when we are falsely accused or blamed?

We wait.

We wait for our Jehovah Jireh to provide.

Are you in a season of waiting on God right now?

1. In our fast today, we will list all the areas we are asking God for provision. Our health, marriage, family, job, joy, contentment.

Where do you need to see God provide in your life?

_____

_____

_____

_____

2. Today we read about David and his struggle with adversity. Enemies, difficulty, and loneliness will always find their way into our lives. Can you remember a time when you felt defeated or discouraged, and God met you in your time of need?

Share that memory below.

_____

_____

_____

_____

3. Abraham knew God would provide for his sacrifice, even though it took an act of faith to see the provision. Stop and look around your circumstance right now. Has God provided a "ram in the thicket" for you? (See previous passage, Gen. 22:13.)

Write down a time God came through in just the perfect moment.

_____

_____

_____

_____

_____

_____

_____

_____

_____

_____

"

When giving, praying, and
fasting are practiced together
in the life of a believer, it
creates a type of threefold
cord that is not easily broken.

Jentezen Franklin

DEAR JEHOVAH JIREH,

I believe You are my Provider. I believe You see the beginning from the end, and You have my well-being in mind.

I ask today in faith that You answer my request. I exercise my belief in You alone and thank You for answering on my behalf.

Thank You for providing the Lamb of God for my salvation.

In Jesus' Name,
Amen

Journal Entry

_____

_____

_____

_____

_____

_____

DAILY PRAYER

day

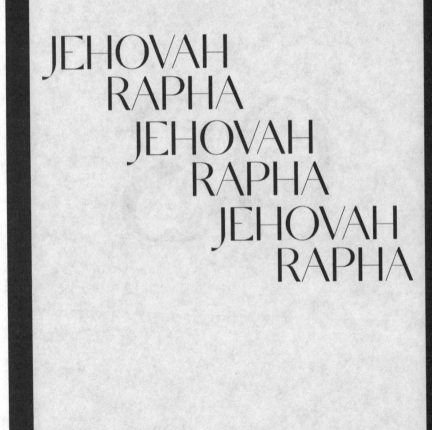

JEHOVAH RAPHA

Jehovah Rapha
(The Lord Who Heals You)

Occurs only once, in Exodus 15:22-27.

Jehovah is another form of YHWH (see Yahweh in Day 2) and means "Lord and Master," as well as "The Existing One." It is the promised and proper name of God.

Rapha means "to heal or make healthy." Together Jehovah Rapha means *"The Lord Who Heals You."*

God is the Great Physician who heals His people. This truth in God's name applies equally to emotional, psychological, and physical healing as well as to the healing of nations.

Exodus 15:22-27:
"So Moses brought Israel from the Red Sea; then they went out into the Wilderness of Shur. And they went three days in the wilderness and found no water. Now when they came to Marah, they could not drink the waters of Marah,

for they *were* bitter. Therefore, the name of it was called Marah. And the people complained against Moses, saying, 'What shall we drink?' So he cried out to the Lord, and the Lord showed him a tree. When he cast *it* into the waters, the waters were made sweet. There He made a statute and an ordinance for them, and there He tested them, and said, 'If you diligently heed the voice of the Lord your God and do what is right in His sight, give ear to His commandments and keep all His statutes, I will put none of the diseases on you which I have brought on the Egyptians. For I *am* the Lord who heals you (Jehovah Rapha).' Then they came to Elim, where there *were* twelve wells of water and seventy palm trees; so, they camped there by the waters."

I love this passage of scripture. Actually, the whole chapter is powerful. In this portion, we read the story of the children of Israel after they had victory over the Egyptians.

They have crossed over the Red Sea safely and sang a song of complete triumph over their enemy.

Yet now, three days later, they are back on the journey going through the wilderness and find no sweet water, only bitter waters. They are not happy campers. Crying out to Moses, they ask, "Where is God now? Has He so quickly forsaken us?"

These waters are Marah-Bitter. Moses turns to God. "What am I to do?" God replies, "Take the tree that is next to you and place it into the waters." Immediately the waters become sweet.

God turned to speak. "This was a test. If you diligently heed the voice of the Lord your God and do what is right in His sight, follow His commandment and statutes, then I will not allow any disease to come upon you. For I Am (Jehovah Rapha) the God that heals you."

Our relationship with God is based on biblical truths. If we violate truth, we bear the consequences of our choices.

The good news is that God is a Healer God, and when pain, brokenness, grief, or disappointment come our way, He is there to heal and forgive.

TODAY'S FASTING FOCUS

FASTING FOR HEALING

Mark 9:23-29:

"Jesus said to him, 'If you can believe, all things *are* possible to him who believes.' Immediately the father of the child cried out and said with tears, 'Lord, I believe; help my unbelief!' When Jesus saw that the people came running together, He rebuked the unclean spirit, saying to it, 'Deaf and dumb spirit, I command you, come out of him and enter him no more!' Then the *spirit* cried out, convulsed him greatly, and came out of him. And he became as one dead, so that many said, 'He is dead.' But Jesus took him by the hand and lifted him up, and he arose. And when He had come into the house, His disciples asked Him privately, 'Why could we not cast it out?' So He said to them, 'This kind can come out by nothing but prayer and fasting.' "

This passage takes us deep in our faith. We all have had moments in our spiritual journey when we try to exercise our faith but to no avail.

We ask, seek, knock, pray and repent, but God seems miles away. I am sure the disciples wondered why they could not cast out this demon.

They had done it before, so why was this time different? After Jesus met with the family of the ailing boy, He asked them, "Do you believe?"

The father responded, "Yes, Lord, I believe, help my unbelief." Jesus, in His compassion, rebuked the demon and reached down and gave the boy His hand to stand up. Later the disciples asked Jesus why they could not cast the demon from the boy. Jesus replied, "This kind can come out by nothing but prayer and fasting."

The truth from this passage is some things need fasting for healing and breakthrough.

Fasting is a powerful weapon to fight the enemy of God.

Read Mark 9:14-29.

1. Have you struggled at times seeing God work on your behalf? You pray and believe, but nothing happens?
Take a moment now and renew your commitment to fasting. Your fast is more than just going without something or giving something up. Your fast is a weapon to do warfare.

_____

_____

_____

_____

2. In the story, we see a father broken over the sickness and mental health of his child. Have you come to God over the pain of a loved one lately? When you find that you can't help and others can't help, turn to Jesus. Take a moment now and renew your faith in God. Exercise your faith and believe in God. See it as your Jehovah Jireh sees it - *provided for.*

Now write a prayer of faith with thanksgiving to God.

_____

_____

_____

_____

3. When Jesus returned with His disciples back in the house, they asked Him a simple question: "Why could we not cast out the demon?" Jesus did not rebuke them or scold them or shame them. He taught them. The lesson was the fact that there is power in fasting. But it was also that Jesus is here to teach and train us. Don't ever feel embarrassed to ask God a question. We are all on a spiritual journey, and the path to truth is one to be learned daily. If you could ask God anything right now, what would it be? Now is your time to ask Him. Spend some time talking with God right now. He has been waiting for this moment.

_____

_____

_____

_____

> "
>
> Our prayers may be awkward.
> Our attempts may be feeble.
> But since the power of prayer
> is in the one who hears it and
> not in the one who says it, our
> prayers do make a difference.
>
> Max Lucado

DAILY PRAYER

DEAR JEHOVAH RAPHA,

You are my Healer. You are the Great Physician. God, I ask that You continue to work in miracles and a supernatural way to bring wholeness and healing to my family and me.

Thank You that You always hear, see, and know my need before I even pray.

Accept my fast today as an act of prayer in gratitude for all Your goodness.

In Jesus' Name,
Amen

Journal Entry

_____

_____

_____

_____

_____

09

JEHOVAH NISSI

Jehovah Nissi (The Lord Is My Banner)

Occurs only once, in Exodus 17:15.

Moses built an altar and called it
The Lord is my Banner (Jehovah Nissi).
Exodus 17:15

As we have seen in previous names,
Jehovah means "The Existing One"
or "Lord." It suggests "to become" or
specifically "to become known" – He is a
God who reveals Himself to be known.

In Hebrew, Nes (nês), from which Nissi is
derived, means "banner."

In Exodus 17:15, Moses acknowledges
that the Lord was Israel's banner under
which they defeated the Amalekites.

He stops and builds an altar unto God
and names it Jehovah Nissi (the Lord our
Banner).

Nes can also be translated as a pole with
a flag attached.

145

In battle, opposing nations would carry their flags on poles at each of their respective front lines.

This was to show the name with which they marched and whose authority they were under.

In this passage, Moses knew their victory came from God alone. The warring tribe of Amalek was strong and fierce. Moses sent Joshua and his men to fight against the Amalekites as he went up to the top of the mountain and raised his arms with the rod of God.

When his arms were lifted high, Israel prevailed. But as he grew weak and lowered his arms, the Amalekites prevailed. One thing this passage teaches us is that there is power in unity and teamwork.

Moses had taken Aaron and Hur with him on top of the mountain. They all realized Moses could not win the battle alone. The two men propped Moses up on a rock and then together lifted his arms in victory.

The battle was won, and Moses built an altar unto God and called it Jehovah Nissi.

I've often wondered if Moses called God his Banner (same word for pole) because he raised the rod of God above his circumstance.

The Lord Our Banner. Just as the rod was raised in power to defeat the enemy, so does the banner you raise unto your Lord conquer the enemy in your daily life.

Raise your banner of power over your circumstance today.

FASTING FOR HUMILITY

Ezra 8:21:

"I proclaimed a fast, so that we might humble ourselves before our God and ask him for a safe journey for us and our children, with all our possessions....So we fasted and petitioned our God about this, and he answered our prayer."

Here, fasting was a means to humility.

God's children humbled themselves before the Lord as they sought protection and safety for themselves and their children.

Let's take a moment and talk about humility. The definition of humility is *a modest or low view of one's own importance.*

In today's world of self-empowerment and self-advancement, it is often difficult to know how to humble ourselves.

Yet this scripture of prayer and fasting

indicates the importance of coming to God in reverence and respect. As you journey through your fast today, stop and ask God for a humble spirit.

Meditate on these passages:

James 4:6:
"But He gives more grace. Therefore He says: 'God resists the proud, but gives grace to the humble.' "

Psalm 25:9:
"The humble He guides in justice, and the humble He teaches His way."

1. In our study today, we saw the word *Nissi* defined as "Banner" or "Pole."

It was something lifted high above all others. Jehovah Nissi is our banner and is to be exalted high above all other gods, passions, desires, and idols.

Is there something you have placed above God? Something that has your attention and devotion more than Him?

Take a moment and write down anything keeping you from truly surrendering all to Him.

_____

_____

_____

_____

2. As we read in our passage today, Moses grew weary and needed help lifting his arms high to win the battle.

We all need accountability and assistance at times.

Who do you have holding you accountable in your life?

List their name here.

_____

_____

_____

_____

3. Today we are fasting for humility and protection. This time of reflection and evaluation could be the very thing to draw you closer to the presence of God.

Meditate on the faithfulness and love that God has shown you. Now write down your personal thank-you declaration to God.

_____

_____

_____

_____

> "
>
> To be a Christian without prayer is no more possible than to be alive without breathing.
>
> Martin Luther

DEAR JEHOVAH NISSI,

Thank You for being My Banner of protection.

Thank You for leading, guiding, and ordaining my steps.

I lift You high above all other gods and call You alone my Lord and Savior.

Your name only is to be praised.

In Jesus' Name,
Amen

Journal Entry

_____

_____

_____

_____

_____

_____

DAILY PRAYER

10

EL QANNA

El Qanna (Jealous God)

Used five times in the Bible.

First seen in Exodus 20:5.

As we have seen, *El* is a name translated as "God" and is often used in conjunction with other words to designate aspects of God's character.

Qanna is translated "jealous," and its meaning relates to a marriage relationship. In this passage, God is depicted as Israel's husband, jealous for His bride.

Let's take a moment and read the passages in the Bible.

"You shall not worship them or serve them; for I, the LORD your God, am a **jealous God (El Qanna)** visiting the iniquity of the fathers on the children, to the third and the fourth generations of those who hate Me,"
Exodus 20:5

"For you shall worship no other god, for the LORD, whose name is **Jealous (El Qanna)**, is a **jealous God**."
Exodus 34:14

"For the LORD your God is a consuming fire, a **jealous God (El Qanna)**."
Deuteronomy 4:24

"Thou shalt not make thee any graven image, or any likeness of any thing that is in heaven above, or that is in the earth beneath, or that is in the waters beneath the earth: Thou shalt not bow down thyself unto them, nor serve them: for I the Lord thy God am a jealous God (El Qanna), visiting the iniquity of the fathers upon the children unto the third and fourth generation of them that hate me."
Deuteronomy 5:8-9

"For the LORD your God in the midst of you is a **jealous God (El Qanna)**; otherwise the anger of the LORD your God will be kindled against you, and He will wipe you off the face of the earth."
Deuteronomy 6:15

Did you know God is jealous for you?

For your love, affection, and admiration?

I know as you read these passages, you probably thought they seemed a little bit possessive, correct? But the truth is, God deserves our love and devotion. God takes this issue so seriously because He knows what happens when we lose our first love. We become adulterous, lusting after the things the world tries to offer us: Money, fame, flirtation, success all try to woo us into a relationship.

But our God says, "Don't be fooled, I love you with an everlasting love, and I am a jealous God. Stay close to Me and stay in My arms of safety."

El Qanna takes His relationship with us seriously, and there are consequences when we violate our commitment. Our choices affect not only us but also the next generation.

You can bless your children and your children's children by simply loving God and staying faithful to Him.

TODAY'S FASTING FOCUS

FASTING FOR RENEWAL

Exodus 34:28:

"So he was there with the Lord forty days and forty nights; he neither ate bread nor drank water. And he wrote on the tablets the words of the covenant, the Ten Commandments."

This story in Exodus 34 is so powerful. Moses was back for a second time to get the Ten Commandments from God.

The first time did not end so well (read Exodus 32). In a very personal and intimate encounter, God met face to face with Moses.

This time the commandments were to be delivered. This is also the chapter we just read about El Qanna.

In Exodus 34:14 God tells Moses, "For thou shalt worship no other god: for the Lord, whose name is Jealous, is a jealous God."

This experience changed Moses forever. Nothing could satisfy his hunger and thirst but God alone. He did not eat bread or drink water for forty days. This moment in history changed not only the physical look of Moses but also the eternal side as well. The Bible says that even Moses' face shown with the glory of God. (Read Exodus 34:29-20.)

Can you imagine an encounter with God as He tells you His top ten commandments for humanity, and one of them is "have no other God before me for I am a jealous God"?

I think I would fast for forty days, too!

Remember, your fast is your prayer and your offering unto God. Take a moment to read Exodus 32-34.

1. Have you ever been jealous over someone? If so, it was probably because you loved them so much and didn't want to share them with another. Today we learned about the great love that God has for His children. How does it make you feel that God loves you so much that He is jealous over you? Take a moment and thank El Qanna for His deep and never-ending love for you. Now ask yourself if you have placed any other gods before El Qanna. If so, are you willing to release them now?

Take a moment and talk with God.

2. Forty days is a long time to fast. Jesus is the only person other than Moses to fast forty days. How is your fast going so far? Has it been more difficult than you thought or a bit easier? The purpose of a fast is to encounter God and bring Him our affection and praise. It is a time to discipline our flesh and have restraint over the things that control us.

Take a moment and journal something you are asking God to do. Is He working?

Ask God to help you through the next half of our fast. We are ten days in, and God is moving in ways you can't even see as of yet!

Journal your thoughts here:

_____

_____

_____

_____

3. Today we are fasting for renewal. Moses became so angry at the children of Israel that he lost his temper and threw the commandments God had given him on the ground. Returning a second time was a another chance for Moses to truly encounter God. Renewal is to make new again. Take a moment today and renew your personal commitment to God. Confess any sin, anger, or issue keeping you from truly being filled with His Spirit. Invite God to be on the throne of your life today.

Share your thoughts here:

_____

_____

_____

_____

> "
>
> It is possible to move men,
> through God, by prayer alone.
>
> Hudson Taylor

DEAR EL QANNA,

Thank You for Your deep love and affection toward me.

I understand You are a jealous God and desire my unconditional devotion.

Today I renew my commitment and vow to You.

I will have no other gods before You.

In Jesus' Name,
Amen

Journal Entry

_____
_____
_____
_____
_____
_____

DAILY PRAYER

11

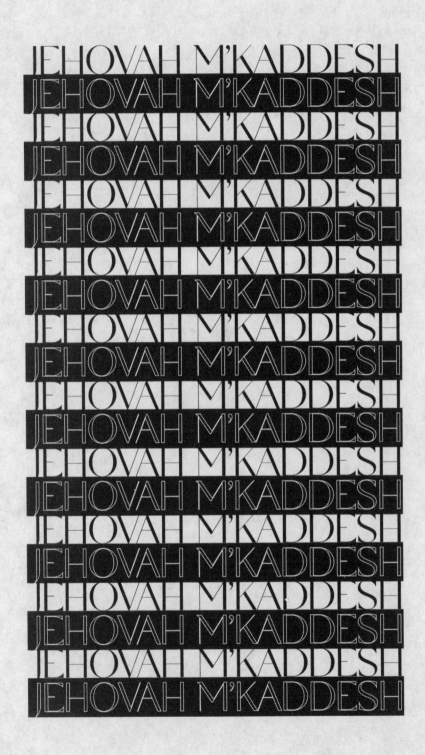

JEHOVAH M'KADDESH

Jehovah M'Kaddesh
(The Lord My Sanctifier)

Is mentioned seven times.

As we have learned, Jehovah means Lord, and the Hebrew word *kaddesh* means "sanctify, consecrate, to set apart as holy." So, Jehovah M'Kaddesh means "The LORD My Sanctifier."

The name Jehovah M'Kaddesh was first given by God to Moses in Exodus 31:13:

"Speak also to the children of Israel, saying: 'Surely My Sabbaths you shall keep, for it is a sign between Me and you throughout your generations, that you may know that I *am* the Lord who sanctifies you (M'Kaddesh).' "

As we learned from our reading yesterday, Moses was on the mountain receiving the Ten Commandments from the Lord and fasting for forty days. The commandment the Lord gave him was to observe the Sabbath.

Observing the Sabbath day would be an agreement between God and His people throughout the generations. God was teaching Moses to teach the people that consecration was a vital part of their relationship. That it is our will that must be given freely through setting aside all other things. I think the fact that God made the Sabbath Day one of His "top ten commandments" tells us a lot about how much He values our attention. For most people, Sunday is the day we set aside for God. We attend church services, worship, give our offering, and fellowship with other believers. God's plan for setting aside a day to be holy is what keeps us grounded and committed. I love the way the passage says, "This will be a sign between Me and you for all generations."

Our decision to make the Sabbath (or Sunday) holy unto the Lord is a witness to generations to come.

One last verse to meditate on about Jehovah M'Kaddesh is:

Leviticus 20:7-8:
"Consecrate yourselves therefore, and be holy, for I *am* the Lord your God. And you shall

keep My statutes and perform them:
I *am* the Lord who sanctifies you (M'Kaddesh)."

God starts with the word consecrate. That means to focus one's attention or mental effort on a particular object or activity.

We are to place our focus and thoughts on Him. He is to be our model for holiness. The promise is that if we keep His commandments and statutes, He will sanctify (use us) for His purpose and will.

We are sanctified at salvation because of the Blood of Jesus, but we must also daily choose to set ourselves apart unto God for His service.

1 Thessalonians 5:23: "Now may the God of peace Himself sanctify you completely; and may your whole spirit, soul, and body be preserved blameless at the coming of our Lord Jesus Christ."

FASTING FOR FAVOR

Nehemiah 1:4:

"And it came to pass, when I heard these words, that I sat down and wept, and mourned certain days, and fasted, and prayed before the God of heaven."

We have all been there, overwhelmed with sorrow and brokenness. That is where we find the prophet Nehemiah in this passage. Word had gotten back to him that "the wall of Jerusalem *was* broken down, and its gates are burned with fire" (verse 3). Nehemiah loved the city of Jerusalem and God's people. They had gone through a rebellious and selfish season, and God had turned away from them. Nehemiah was seeking repentance and forgiveness on behalf of Israel.

Read Nehemiah 1:1-11:
"The words of Nehemiah the son of Hachaliah. It came to pass in the month of Chislev, *in* the twentieth year, as I was in Shushan the citadel, that Hanani

one of my brethren came with men from
Judah; and I asked them concerning the
Jews who had escaped, who had survived
the captivity, and concerning Jerusalem. And
they said to me, 'The survivors who are left
from the captivity in the province *are* there
in great distress and reproach. The wall of
Jerusalem *is* also broken down, and its gates
are burned with fire.' So it was, when I heard
these words, that I sat down and wept, and
mourned *for many* days; I was fasting and
praying before the God of heaven. And I said: 'I
pray, Lord God of heaven, O great and awesome
God, *You* who keep *Your* covenant and mercy
with those who love You and observe our
commandments, please let Your ear be attentive
and Your eyes open, that You may hear the
prayer of Your servant which I pray before
You now, day and night, for the children of
Israel Your servants, and confess the sins of
the children of Israel which we have sinned
against You. Both my father's house and I have
sinned. We have acted very corruptly against
You, and have not kept the commandments,
the statutes, nor the ordinances which You
commanded Your servant Moses. Remember,
I pray, the word that You commanded Your
servant Moses, saying, "*If* you are unfaithful, I

will scatter you among the nations; but *if* you return to Me, and keep My commandments and do them, though some of you were cast out to the farthest part of the heavens, *yet* I will gather them from there, and bring them to the place which I have chosen as a dwelling for My name." Now these *are* Your servants and Your people, whom You have redeemed by Your great power, and by Your strong hand. O Lord, I pray, please let Your ear be attentive to the prayer of Your servant, and to the prayer of Your servants who desire to fear Your name; and let Your servant prosper this day, I pray, and grant him mercy in the sight of this man.' For I was the king's cupbearer."

Nehemiah was fasting for favor from the King.

He desired to go back to Jerusalem and rebuild the city walls.

It would take divine favor for the King to agree to such a request.

And that is exactly what the power of fasting can do. It gets God's attention and man's favor.

1. Today we learned about Jehovah M'Kaddesh, the God who sanctifies. Our sanctification is a gift from God. It cannot be bought or earned. It, like salvation, is a free gift. But as discussed, we too must live a life where we set ourselves apart for a holy purpose. We must strive to live a sanctified life.

What do you need to lay down and crucify to God today? Pride, anger, fear, doubt? Take a moment and write down anything keeping you from being completely surrendered.

_____

_____

_____

_____

2. Nehemiah was at a place of complete surrender. His heart broke for the people of Israel. They had left their first love.

Did you notice what his first response to the news was? He wept and mourned and fasted. He got right with God and then prayed for the people to repent.

If you want to see a breakthrough in your life, you must start by examining your heart. When was the last time you wept and mourned over your sin?

Take a moment now to reevaluate your life. Is there anything keeping you from making a request to the King? King Jesus!

Write down your thoughts here:

_____

_____

_____

_____

3. Now that you are ready, what request would you like to make to the King? It could not have been easy for Nehemiah to approach the King with a request to return to Jerusalem to rebuild the temple. It took courage and faith to be so bold, and he asked for favor.

What would you like to ask God to do for you?

_____

_____

_____

_____

> "
>
> To get nations back on their feet, we must first get down on our knees.
>
> Billy Graham

DEAR JEHOVAH M'KADDESH,

You require that I remember the Sabbath Day and keep it as a sign to all generations.

Today I renew my commitment to You and thank You for the free gift of sanctification.

Thank You for making me holy in Your sight.

In Jesus' Name,
Amen

Journal Entry

_____

_____

_____

_____

_____

DAILY PRAYER

JEHOVAH SHALOM

JEHOVAH SHALOM

Jehovah Shalom (The Lord Is Peace)

Occurs only once, in Judges 6:24.

"So Gideon built an altar to the Lord there and called it The Lord Is Peace. To this day it stands in Ophrah of the Abiezrites."
Judges 6:24

If there ever was a man that needed a sign, it was Gideon.

In Judges 6, we read the story of God's angel coming face to face with Gideon.

Once again, God's children had walked away from Him, turning to worship Baal and foreign gods.

But in God's grace and mercy, He sent His angel to prepare Gideon for an encounter.

At the time, Gideon was hiding from his enemy. The angel spoke up and said, "The Lord *is* with you, you mighty man of valor!"

I'm sure Gideon thought he had the wrong person.

Me? he thought.

"Yes," said the angel. "God is going to use you in battle." "If this is true, show me a sign."

As he requested, the angel gave him a sign.

Judges 6:21-24:
"Then the Angel of the Lord put out the end of the staff that *was* in His hand and touched the meat and the unleavened bread; and fire rose out of the rock and consumed the meat and the unleavened bread. And the Angel of the Lord departed out of his sight.
Now Gideon perceived that He *was* the Angel of the Lord. So Gideon said, 'Alas, O Lord God! For I have seen the Angel of the Lord face to face.' Then the Lord said to him, 'Peace be with you; do not fear, you shall not die.'
So Gideon built an altar there to the Lord and called it The-Lord-Is-Peace."

All it took was the Lord speaking peace over him to change his outlook from fear to peace. Jehovah Shalom brings peace.

Remember, when you feel like a failure and coward, Jehovah God, Jehovah Shalom, is your guide.

Gideon built an altar unto the Lord to show his honor and respect for the encounter.

FASTING FOR PEACE

2 Sam. 12:16-17:

"David therefore pleaded with God for the child, and David fasted and went in and lay all night on the ground. So the elders of his house arose *and went* to him, to raise him up from the ground. But he would not, nor did he eat food with them."

In 2 Samuel 12, we read the story of the consequences of a bad decision. King David had let his fleshly affection for Bathsheba go too far, and now he was dealing with God's judgment. David powered up and used his position as King to seduce a married woman.

He knew better, but his pride was leading his reason. Bathsheba became pregnant and had a son who was fighting for his life. David repents of his action and turns to God in prayer and fasting. "Oh God, forgive my ways and heal my son." David's son does not live. After hearing the news, he goes and washes and anoints himself.

"When David saw that his servants were whispering, David perceived that the child was dead. Therefore, David said to his servants, 'Is the child dead?' And they said, 'He is dead.' So David arose from the ground, washed, and anointed himself, and changed his clothes; and he went into the house of the Lord and worshiped."
2 Samuel 12:19-20

God was not finished with David and Bathsheba, for shortly after this experience, Bathsheba becomes pregnant with Solomon, the next-to-be King of Israel.

You see, God has a way of making all things new. With time and healing, our Jehovah Shalom brings peace and unity.

There are times when God's ways are higher than ours. They don't make sense and can even bring grief.

Those are the times to cry out to Jehovah Shalom for peace and understanding. He can make a way where there seems to be no way.

1. Have you ever asked God to show you a sign? For Gideon, it was a regular occurrence. Not only did he ask the Angel for a sign in Judges 6:17, but also again with the fleece in Judges 6:37-40.

What sign are you asking God for today?

_____

_____

_____

_____

2. Gideon was anything but a warrior, yet the Angel of God saw something in him other than fear. He saw potential.

God also sees more in you than you see in yourself. What view of yourself are you struggling with today that is not from God? (failure, dumb, quitter, defeated)

How does God see you? List it here:

_____

_____

_____

3. Today we read about the failure and loss of
a mighty King. Even King David made poor
decisions at times. Yet Jehovah Shalom brought
a new beginning and a fresh start. Where do
you need a fresh start? Where do you need the
Prince of Peace to comfort and restore you?

Write a prayer to God for a present-day filling of
His Spirit and that His peace would guard your
heart and your mind in Christ Jesus.

_____

_____

_____

_____

> " "
> Prayer is not monologue, but dialogue; God's voice is its most essential part. Listening to God's voice is the secret of the assurance that He will listen to mine.
>
> Andrew Murray

DEAR JEHOVAH SHALOM,

Your Peace is incomparable.

Nothing this world has to offer can soothe my heart and comfort my soul like Your presence.

I ask that You take my circumstances and difficulties and exchange them for Your Divine Peace. I thank You for the Joy of the Lord in my life.

In Jesus' Name,
Amen

Journal Entry

_____

_____

_____

_____

_____

_____

DAILY PRAYER

day

JEHOVAH
SABAOTH

JEHOVAH SABAOTH

Jehovah Sabaoth (The Lord of Hosts)

First seen in 1 Samuel 1:3.

Used in the Bible more than 285 times.

"This man went up from his city yearly to worship and sacrifice to the Lord of hosts in Shiloh. Also the two sons of Eli, Hophni and Phinehas, the priests of the Lord, were there." 1 Samuel 1:3

As we have learned, Jehovah is translated as "The Existing One" or "Lord." The meaning of Jehovah comes from the Hebrew word Havah, meaning "to be" or "to exist." Sabaoth (se bâ'ôt) means "armies" or "hosts." Jehovah Sabaoth can be translated as "The Lord of Armies" (1 Samuel 1:3). This name denotes His universal power and sovereignty over every army, both spiritual and earthly. The Lord of Hosts is the King of all Heaven and earth. (Psalm 24:9-10; Psalm 84:3; Isaiah 6:5)

This story in 1 Samuel demonstrates the power of God. A man named

Elkanah had two wives. We do not know the circumstance behind why two wives, but we do know he was a responsible husband. The scripture tells us he went up yearly to the house of God to worship and sacrifice to the Lord.

The scripture (1 Samuel 1:4-5) goes on to say:

"And whenever the time came for Elkanah to make an offering, he would give portions to Peninnah his wife and to all her sons and daughters. But to Hannah he would give a double portion, for he loved Hannah, although the Lord had closed her womb."

In this passage, we read about the brokenness of a barren woman. Hannah desired a child more than anything. In verse eleven, she cried out to God with a vow:

"Then she made a vow and said, O Lord of hosts, if You will indeed look on the affliction of Your maidservant and remember me, and not forget Your maidservant, but will give Your maidservant a male child, then I will give him to the Lord all the days of his life, and no razor shall come upon his head."

The Priest Eli overheard her prayer in verse 17:

"Then Eli answered and said, 'Go in peace,
and the God of Israel grant your petition which
you have asked of Him.'

"And she said, 'Let your maidservant find favor
in your sight.' So the woman went her way and
ate, and her face was no longer *sad*."

Hannah trusted in the Lord of Hosts. The Lord
of Armies. God came through with her request,
and Hannah gave birth to the prophet Samuel.

Not only did Elkanah worship Jehovah Sabaoth,
but Hannah also called out to The Lord of Hosts.

Where do you need The Lord of Angels to
guard you today?

Cry out to our Jehovah Sabaoth.

TODAY'S FASTING FOCUS

A CALL TO REPENTANCE

Joel 1:14:

"Consecrate a fast, call a sacred assembly; gather the elders *and* all the inhabitants of the land *into* the house of the Lord your God, and cry out to the Lord."

Joel 2:12:

" 'Now, therefore,' says the Lord, 'turn to Me with all your heart, with fasting, with weeping, and with mourning.' "

There is not a more telling passage to show the rebellion and disobedience of the children of God than this one in Joel. The people had turned away from God, and their hearts had hardened.

The prophet had sounded the alarm and called for a holy assembly. Could this be the same story for us today? As we stop and reflect on today's passage, let me encourage you to consider your heart attitude and spiritual condition.

Our twenty-one-day fast is a time to meditate and intentionally draw close to God.

Twice in these two passages, the Prophet pleads with the people to mourn, cry aloud, and turn their hearts to the Lord.

Today's fasting focus is on repentance.

Is there anything in your life right now that you need to confess and give over to God?

Today we learned about Jehovah Sabaoth.

The Lord of Hosts.

As Hannah called out to God, she encountered the Prophet of God asking her what she wanted.

She replied in no uncertain terms what her request was.

If you were confronted with that opportunity, would you be able to articulate your request?

1. What would you ask God to do for you?

Write your reply to God here:

_____

_____

_____

_____

2. Read Joel 1 and 2.
What was something God showed you through
this passage?

_____

_____

_____

_____

3. What things do you see today that are similar
to the days of the Prophets?

_____

_____

_____

_____

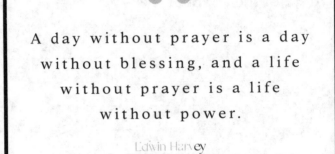

A day without prayer is a day without blessing, and a life without prayer is a life without power.

Edwin Harvey

DAILY PRAYER

DEAR JEHOVAH SABAOTH,

I trust You as my Lord of Armies.

I believe I am surrounded and protected by Your loving arms. Today I bring my request to You and believe by faith You have heard me and will answer me.

Thank You for being my Lord of Hosts.

In Jesus' Name,
Amen

Journal Entry

_____
_____
_____
_____
_____

EL DEAH EL DEAH EL DEAH EL DEAH EL DEAH EL DEAH EL DEAH
EL DEAH EL DEAH EL DEAH EL DEAH EL DEAH EL DEAH EL DEAH
EL DEAH EL DEAH EL DEAH EL DEAH EL DEAH EL DEAH EL DEAH
EL DEAH EL DEAH EL DEAH EL DEAH EL DEAH EL DEAH EL DEAH
EL DEAH EL DEAH EL DEAH EL DEAH EL DEAH EL DEAH EL DEAH
EL DEAH EL DEAH EL DEAH EL DEAH EL DEAH EL DEAH EL DEAH
EL DEAH EL DEAH EL DEAH EL DEAH EL DEAH EL DEAH EL DEAH
EL DEAH EL DEAH EL DEAH EL DEAH EL DEAH EL DEAH EL DEAH
EL DEAH EL DEAH EL DEAH EL DEAH EL DEAH EL DEAH EL DEAH
EL DEAH EL DEAH EL DEAH EL DEAH EL DEAH EL DEAH EL DEAH

EL DEAH

EL DEAH EL DEAH EL DEAH EL DEAH EL DEAH EL DEAH EL DEAH
EL DEAH EL DEAH EL DEAH EL DEAH EL DEAH EL DEAH EL DEAH
EL DEAH EL DEAH EL DEAH EL DEAH EL DEAH EL DEAH EL DEAH
EL DEAH EL DEAH EL DEAH EL DEAH EL DEAH EL DEAH EL DEAH
EL DEAH EL DEAH EL DEAH EL DEAH EL DEAH EL DEAH EL DEAH
EL DEAH EL DEAH EL DEAH EL DEAH EL DEAH EL DEAH EL DEAH
EL DEAH EL DEAH EL DEAH EL DEAH EL DEAH EL DEAH EL DEAH
EL DEAH EL DEAH EL DEAH EL DEAH EL DEAH EL DEAH EL DEAH
EL DEAH EL DEAH EL DEAH EL DEAH EL DEAH EL DEAH EL DEAH
EL DEAH EL DEAH EL DEAH EL DEAH EL DEAH EL DEAH EL DEAH

El Deah (God of Knowledge)

First seen in 1 Samuel 2:3.

"Talk no more so very proudly; let no arrogance come from your mouth, for the Lord *is* the God of knowledge; and by Him actions are weighed."

We pick up the story of Hannah in today's reading. Not only did Hannah experience the Lord of Hosts, El Sabaoth, but now she encounters The God of Knowledge, El Deah.

God in His foreknowledge knew the outcome of Hannah's prayer.

God had a plan because God is omniscient. He knows everything.

God is the God of all knowledge. God sees the beginning. God sees the middle. God sees the end. God sees it all at one time. God is all-knowing.

There is nothing that takes Him by surprise.

EL DEAH

Hannah's prayer became her praise.

This passage acknowledges the all-powerful and all-knowing God of the universe. He is El Deah.

Hannah had been ridiculed and belittled by her adversary for far too long.

Now The God of Knowledge was vindicating her cause.

In Romans 11:33, we read:

"Oh, the depth of the riches both of the wisdom and knowledge of God! How unsearchable *are* His judgments and His ways past finding out!"

God knows your pain, your plea, your proposal.

Today, take a moment to hear from El Deah, your God of Knowledge.

Ask Him to lead you on paths of righteousness and direct you in divine discourses.

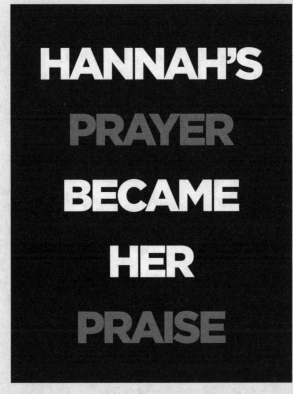

FASTING FOR WISDOM AND KNOWLEDGE

Daniel 9:3-5:

"Then I set my face toward the Lord God to make request by prayer and supplications, with fasting, sackcloth, and ashes. And I prayed to the Lord my God, and made confession, and said, 'O Lord, great and awesome God, who keeps His covenant and mercy with those who love Him, and with those who keep His commandments, we have sinned and committed iniquity, we have done wickedly and rebelled, even by departing from Your precepts and Your judgments.' "
(Read the entire chapter.)

Daniel is an intriguing and prophetic book. God's people have been taken captive by the Babylonians for seventy years, and Daniel was chosen to be the mouthpiece for God. Through dreams, visions, and prophetic prayer, God used him to reveal what would happen in the future.

Daniel was a man of faith and leadership; no wonder God could trust him with inspiration and revelation. In our passage today, Daniel calls the people to seek wisdom and knowledge from God.

When we depart from God's ways, we must turn back by admitting our rebellion and independence from Him.

God desires to give us His wisdom and insights, but we must be filled with His power to do so.

Look what Daniel said in verse 3:
"Then I set my face toward the Lord God to make request by prayer and supplications, with fasting, sackcloth, and ashes."

Daniel set his face toward God. How many times do we turn away when we are confronted with a truth we don't want to admit?

Yet here we see the heart of this leader. Face forward and fully committed to the authority of God, Daniel prayed to his God.

Both through fasting and repentance (the act of sackcloth and ashes), he surrendered to God.

1. Today we learned about El Deah, the All-Knowing God. Sometimes we think we can hide from God and go our own way. But the truth is, He is omniscient (All-Knowing). It is like a small child hiding under a lace tablecloth and then saying, "Come try to find me," not realizing everything is exposed.

Is there something you are hiding from God today? Spoiler alert: He already knows. Take a moment and write down anything you feel needs to be addressed with God. The conversation will be freeing, believe me.

_____

_____

_____

_____

2. Hannah had been belittled and ridiculed for not being able to conceive. The pain was real. Have you had something said about you that has broken your spirit and kept you in bondage? God hears your cry and can heal your heart.

Share a painful memory or lie that the enemy has used to keep you from the freedom God has for you.

_____

_____

_____

_____

3. Today we learned that Daniel "set his face" toward God. Fasting is an act of faith to see God move in our lives. It is not for show or sympathy. It is for breakthrough. Take some time right now to "set your face toward God." What do you see? Don't ever be afraid to look into the face of Jesus. You may need to do some course correction, but the process will leave you wanting more of Him.

What do you see?

_____

_____

_____

_____

> "
>
> Quit playing, start praying.
> Quit feasting, start fasting.
> Talk less with men, talk more
> with God. Listen less to men,
> listen to the words of God.
> Skip travel, start travail.
>
> Leonard Ravenhill

DEAR EL DEAH,

I acknowledge You are the All-Knowing God.

Thank You for Your protection and watchcare over my life.

Teach me to trust Your plans and purpose on my daily journey.

In Jesus' Name,
Amen

Journal Entry

_____
_____
_____
_____
_____
_____

DAILY PRAYER

Jehovah Ra'ah
(The Lord Is My Shepherd)

This name only occurs once, in
Psalm 23:1.

"The Lord *is* my shepherd; I shall
not want."
Psalm 23:1

Ra'ah means to tend, to shepherd, to
feed; to be a special friend.

(Ra'ah is also used as a reference to
God in Genesis 48:15, Genesis 49:24,
and Psalm 80:1.)

As you read Psalm 23, note the phrases
in the psalm that speak of the Lord as
our...

- **NURTURER**
- **PROVIDER**
- **GUIDE**
- **PROTECTOR**
- **FRIEND**

JEHOVAH RA'AH

Psalm 23

"The Lord *is* my shepherd; I shall not want.
He makes me to lie down in green pastures; He
leads me beside the still waters. He restores my
soul; He leads me in the paths of righteousness
for His name's sake. Yea, though I walk through
the valley of the shadow of death, I will fear
no evil; for You *are* with me; Your rod and Your
staff, they comfort me. You prepare a table
before me in the presence of my enemies;
You anoint my head with oil; My cup runs over.
Surely goodness and mercy shall follow me all
the days of my life; and I will dwell in the house
of the Lord forever."

The Lord our Shepherd. Many of us are familiar
with this name of God. Psalm 23 has been
quoted, memorized, and prayed for centuries.

But I hope to share a bit more of the meaning of
this name for you today.

King David, the shepherd boy, knew Jehovah
Ra'ah quite well. Many nights alone on the
mountainside or in the valley, I'm sure he called
out for God to be his Shepherd.

David had firsthand knowledge of his Shepherd.

He declared goodness and mercy over all the days of his life. He chose to "dwell in the house of the Lord forever." He declared his kingship by prophesying, "You anoint my head with oil."

Can you see how important it is to release prophetic words over your life? It is powerful to allow the Good Shepherd to take you by the hand and lead you on the journey.

This psalm would comfort the heart and direct the steps of this soon-to-be king. This shepherd experience would be the very foundation on which God would use David to lead His people.

God uses the things of our past to shape and prepare us for His assignment.

This shepherd boy knew Jehovah Ra'ah personally.

Jehovah Ra'ah is your Shepherd, but He is also your Friend.

FASTING FOR HELP

2 Chronicles 20:3-4

"And Jehoshaphat feared, and set himself to seek the Lord, and proclaimed a fast throughout all Judah. So Judah gathered together to ask *help* from the Lord; and from all the cities of Judah they came to seek the Lord."

In this story, we find the key to victory, and Jehoshaphat did something really wise.

He recounted all the help and assistance God had given them over the years.

He reminded the people of God's provision. Then as they entered a time of prayer and fasting, the Spirit of God fell on Jahaziel.

"And he said, 'Listen, all you of Judah and you inhabitants of Jerusalem, and you, King Jehoshaphat! Thus says the Lord to you: "Do not be

afraid nor dismayed because of this great
multitude, for the battle *is* not yours,
but God's. You will not *need* to fight in
this *battle.* Position yourselves, stand still and
see the salvation of the Lord, who is with you,
O Judah and Jerusalem!" Do not fear or be
dismayed; tomorrow go out against them, for
the Lord *is* with you.' "

The key to victory is asking God for help and
then letting Him act.

"Now when they began to sing and to
praise, the Lord set ambushes against the
people of Ammon, Moab, and Mount Seir,
who had come against Judah; and they were
defeated. For the people of Ammon and Moab
stood up against the inhabitants of Mount Seir
to utterly kill and destroy *them.* And when
they had made an end of the inhabitants of
Seir, they helped to destroy one another."

Your enemies will turn on one another if you will
just stay out of the way.

God will make a way where there seems to be
no way.

1. Read Psalm 23 out loud.
What is God showing you from this chapter?

_____

_____

_____

_____

2. "Ra'ah" means Shepherd, but it also means special friend. Proverbs 18:24 says, "A man *who has* friends must himself be friendly, but there is a friend *who* sticks closer than a brother."

Jesus is the closest friend you will ever have. He will not leave you or forsake you. Now that's a shepherd.

Do you feel yourself wandering off from God at times?

Do the temptations and trials of this world cause you to look away?

Take a moment and allow God's Spirit to draw you back into His fold.

He is the Good Shepherd.

_____

_____

_____

_____

3. One thing we learned about Jehoshaphat was that he recounted the times God was there for him in his need.

Take a few minutes and list some times when God was there for you.

a. _____

b. _____

c. _____

d. _____

> "
>
> Beware in your prayers, above everything else, of limiting God, not only by unbelief, but by fancying that you know what He can do. Expect unexpected things "above all that we ask or think."
>
> Andrew Murray

DEAR JEHOVAH RA'AH,

Thank You that I can rest in Your loving care.

Thank You for leading me in righteousness.

Thank You for restoring my soul.

Thank You for being my Friend.

In Jesus' Name,
Amen

Journal Entry

_____

_____

_____

_____

_____

_____

DAILY PRAYER

El Moshaah
(God of Salvation, God the Deliverer)

This only occurs once, in Psalm 68:19-20.

"Blessed *be* the Lord, *who* daily loads us *with benefits*, the God of our salvation! *Selah*, Our God *is* the God of salvation; and to God the Lord *belong* escapes from death."

Moshaah means "saves."

He is the God who saves!

Have you ever noticed the word *Selah* after a Scripture in the Bible?

Do you know what it means?

Selah means "to stop and consider," "to ponder and reflect." It also means forever.

I love that David put *Selah* right after verse 19. "Blessed be the Lord, who daily loads us with benefits, the God of our Salvation! *Selah*."

EL MOSHAAH

231

El Moshaah loads us with benefits, and salvation is the greatest benefit you will ever receive.

The definition of "benefit" is an advantage, payment, or gift given.

That's what Salvation is, an advantage, a payment, a gift given.

David understood he needed saving.

I'm sure he cried out to El Moshaah many times to rescue and save him.

Our God removes the sting of death and gives us eternal life through salvation.

(First Corinthians 15:55: "O Death, where is your sting? O Hades, where is your victory?")

Have you considered the value of your salvation?

It is loaded with benefits.

Here are a few to think about:

- ## THE JOY OF THE LORD

- ## POWER IN THE HOLY SPIRIT

- ## ETERNAL LIFE

- ## RELATIONSHIP WITH GOD

Wow! Now those are great benefits!

FASTING FOR FAITH

Esther 4:15-16:

"Then Esther told *them* to reply to Mordecai: 'Go, gather all the Jews who are present in Shushan, and fast for me; neither eat nor drink for three days, night or day. My maids and I will fast likewise. And so I will go to the king, which *is* against the law; and if I perish, I perish!' "

What a story of Faith. This account in history is one to remember. A young, unassuming woman was chosen by God to be the Queen of His people for such a time as this. Not only was Esther hand-picked by God, but she was empowered by His mighty hand to stand strong in a time of testing. The situation Esther found herself in was that the King's right-hand man was working behind the scenes to set a trap to kill all the Jews and rid them of their existence. Esther's uncle, Mordecai, had overheard a conversation with the King and his assistant Haman. The King was unaware

234

that his queen (Esther) was Jewish and went along with the recommendation of Haman. What he didn't know was that God knows the plans of all men and will always protect and provide for His people. This is what we call "an Esther moment." For such a time as this. Uncle Mordecai wrote Esther back with these words: "For if you remain silent at this time, relief and deliverance for the Jews will arise from another place, but you and your father's family will perish. And who knows but that you have come to your royal position for such a time as this?"

Esther knew she had to call on the people to pray and fast. Some things only happen by prayer AND fasting. ("However, this kind does not go out except by prayer and fasting." Matthew 7:21)

As God would have it, the very fate Haman planned for Uncle Mordecai (death by hanging) was turned around by the King to be used on Haman. God's people, the Jews, were saved by Queen Esther's act of courage, along with her cry for prayer and fasting. Fasting is a powerful weapon and turns the heart of God toward the heart of those that ask.

1. Today we looked at the name El Moshaah, The God of Salvation. We learned that there are benefits that come with our salvation.

Take some time and list the benefits you have found in your salvation.

a. _____

b. _____

c. _____

d. _____

2. Esther had been born for such a time as this. We all have. God appointed the day you were born with purpose, and on purpose.

Share a "for such a time as this" moment you have had in your life—a Divine God encounter or an opportunity you have had in your life.

_____

_____

_____

_____

3. It took great faith and courage for Esther to approach the King with her request. She knew that telling the people to pray and fast for her was the key to her success.

Have you asked anyone to fast with you for your prayer request?

What are you asking God for today?

_____

_____

_____

_____

"

Every great movement of
God can be traced to a
kneeling figure.

D. L. Moody

DEAR EL MOSHAAH,

Thank You for *all Your* benefits.

You are the God of my salvation!

Thank You for providing protection and watchcare to me on a daily basis.

In Jesus' Name,
Amen

Journal Entry

_____
_____
_____
_____
_____
_____

DAILY PRAYER

JEHOVAH TSIDKENU

Jehovah Tsidkenu
(The Lord Our Righteousness)

Jehovah Tsidkenu is first seen in Jeremiah 23:6.

The only other occurrence is in Jeremiah 33:16.

Jehovah Tsidkenu. We know *Jehovah* is the personal name of God, which is translated as "LORD." *Tsidkenu* means "our righteousness." Altogether *Jehovah Tsidkenu* means "the LORD our righteousness" in Hebrew.

"In His days Judah will be saved, and Israel will dwell safely; now this *is* His name by which He will be called: THE LORD OUR RIGHTEOUSNESS."
Jeremiah 23:6

"In those days Judah will be saved, and Jerusalem will dwell safely. And this *is the name* by which she will be called: THE LORD OUR RIGHTEOUSNESS."
Jeremiah 33:16

The prophet Jeremiah had watched the Children of Israel walk away from God. They had turned to idols and foreign gods and forsaken the one and only true relationship worth having. He began to preach and declare the righteousness of God.

Within every soul is the desire for righteousness (right standing with God). We know from the scripture that our righteousness is but filthy rags (Isaiah 64:6).

So how can I be righteous before a Holy God? Through Jehovah Tsidkenu, Our Righteousness. This passage is foreshadowing the coming Messiah Jesus Himself. It is a promise that although we all stray at times, our righteousness is found in God alone.

It is a promise of righteousness before a Holy God. "How can this be?" you may ask. Well, the verse prior to this promise explains it all.

Jeremiah 33:3:
"Call to Me, and I will answer you, and show you great and mighty things, which you do not know."

We are to call out to God and allow Him to answer us. He promised to show us great and mighty things that we could never know or understand without Him.

His righteousness is one of those things. How can an unrighteous person be righteous? The blood and forgiveness of Jesus, that's how.

He gives us His righteousness as a free gift of salvation.

One more thing we should address before moving on: in 1 John 2:29, the scripture says:

"If you know that He is righteous, you know that everyone who practices righteousness is born of Him."

When you have a personal relationship with Jesus Christ, you have His righteousness because He lives in you.

You are to act and react with the power of the Holy Spirit living in you.

FASTING FOR PROTECTION

Psalm 35:13:

"But as for me, when they were sick, My clothing *was* sackcloth; I humbled myself with fasting..."

The Bible tells us David was a man after the heart of God (1 Samuel 13:14). He longed for the goodness and righteousness of God.

Our fasting passage today shows the kind of man David was. While his enemy pursued him and hunted him down to kill him, he asked God, "Why?"

He reminds God that when they were sick, he humbled himself and fasted for them.

They tried to destroy him, yet he mourned and fasted for them.

Finally, when he had had enough, he asked God to fight against those who fought against him.

David is seeking God's salvation and his enemies' destruction.

Fasting can be a healthy way to reconcile relationships. When you feel others are taking advantage of you or hunting you down to harm you, maybe it's time to fast for them. We see the real and vulnerable side of David in this passage.

The truth is, sometimes we just want God to vindicate us from our enemies.

The key is to be real with God.

As you read today's psalm, notice how God allows David to vent and gripe and then brings him full circle to praising God for His mighty protection and deliverance.

1. Today we meet Jehovah Tsidkenu, Our Righteousness. Many of us grew up believing if we were just good enough, were kind enough, or gave enough, we would go to heaven. But the truth is, we are not enough - not without Jesus, our Righteousness. What Jesus did on the cross made way for us to receive forgiveness and Eternal Life.

The question is, have you experienced that Grace? Have you prayed and asked Him into your life? If so, take some time to thank Him for His gift of Righteousness and Salvation.

Jesus, thank You for...

_____

_____

_____

_____

If you have not trusted in the love and forgiveness of Jesus, here are the steps to Salvation.

See Appendix in the back of the guide.

2. The Bible tells us in Jeremiah 33:3, "Call to Me, and I will answer you, and show you great and mighty things, which you do not know." God has a way of making paths through the wilderness and ways in the desert. What do you need to see God do in your life today that seems like a great and mighty thing?

_____

_____

_____

_____

3. David was tired of running from his enemy. He had shown them kindness and mercy by fasting on their behalf, but to no avail. Now he was done. Is there someone you have gone the extra mile for, yet you still feel unappreciated? David had to turn it over to God. Maybe today is your day to release the conflict to God. In the space below, take a few moments to write your thoughts to God. And then, like David, begin to praise God for His continued watchcare and guidance.

_____

_____

_____

_____

> **"**
>
> All I know is that when I
> pray, coincidences happen;
> and when I don't pray, they
> don't happen.
>
> Dan Hayes

DEAR JEHOVAH TSIDKENU,

Thank You! For out of Your grace, mercy, and love, I am made righteous because of the Cross.

Thank You for the free gift of salvation.

In Jesus' Name,
Amen

Journal Entry

_____

_____

_____

_____

_____

_____

DAILY PRAYER

day

JEHOVAH

SHAMMAH

JEHOVAH SHAMMAH

Jehovah Shammah (The Lord Is There)

This occurs only once, in Ezekiel 48:35.

Ezekiel 48:35:
"All the way around *shall* be eighteen thousand *cubits*; and the name of the city from *that* day *shall be*: THE LORD *IS* THERE."

Ezekiel is a fascinating book filled with prophecy and revelation. In our passage today, we see the prophetic vision Ezekiel gives of the completion of the temple and the powerful name of God - Jehovah Shammah, The Lord is There. The children of God have once again wandered away and are now in captivity.

The powerful and prophetic voice of Ezekiel reminds them God has a plan and He will once again restore His temple.

Verse 35 is the final word after the instruction to each tribe. In his vision, the temple is complete, and the name of the city from that day forward will be...

THE LORD IS THERE! How comforting to know that Jehovah Shammah is there. Always and forever.

These words must have been comforting to the Children of Israel.

Ezekiel's vision was given on the 25th anniversary of his exile and fourteen years after the fall of Jerusalem.

It had been twelve years since they had heard a message of hope in chapter thirty-nine.

Yet now they are reminded Jehovah Shammah is here. He is always there!

FASTING FOR A BROKEN SPIRIT

2 Samuel 1:11:

"Therefore David took hold of his own clothes and tore them, and *so did* all the men who *were* with him. And they mourned and wept and fasted until evening for Saul and for Jonathan his son, for the people of the Lord and for the house of Israel, because they had fallen by the sword."

The Lord is there. Even in times of confusion and discouragement. David had just heard the news that King Saul and his son Jonathan had been killed. This verse shows the compassion and honor David had for authority. Saul was not kind to David, yet he knew how to respect the position of a leader.

Jonathan, however, was another story. David and Jonathan were friends and companions.

Hearing about the death of a friend is never easy, but the way David heard this news and the way it was done caused him to take matters into his own hands. First off, he tore his clothes (a sign of brokenness and grief); next he mourned, wept, and fasted. Did you notice the list of what he fasted for?

Saul, Jonathan, the people, and the house of Israel. It is important when you fast to know what you are fasting for.

Be specific and be intentional. David was grieving, and he was angry.

Sometimes we fast for healing or a miracle, but there are times we fast because of brokenness.

1. Ezekiel introduces us to the name of God – Jehovah Shammah, The Lord is There. Throughout all the years of captivity, Israel hoped that God would come and redeem them.

The prophet's words were not only comforting but empowering to help them make it through the struggle.

Has there been a time when you felt the presence of God through a particular trial?

Share your memory below.

_____

_____

_____

_____

2. Today we looked at the story of David upon hearing the news of King Saul's and Jonathan's deaths. David was brokenhearted and grieving.

What is something weighing heavy on your heart today?

Have you considered fasting for it?
Sometimes it's healthy to write down our
struggles and see them on paper. Take a
moment and write your burden here.

_____

_____

_____

_____

3. We have journeyed together for many days
now. Take a moment and reflect upon your fast
thus far.

What are a few of the things you have been
fasting for?

List them below.

_____

_____

_____

_____

> "
>
> Prayer is not overcoming God's reluctance, but laying hold of His willingness.
>
> Martin Luther

DAILY PRAYER

DEAR JEHOVAH SHAMMAH,

Thank You for always being there. In good times and bad You are always there.

I trust You know how to lead and guide the steps of my life.

Please teach me to follow Your ways.

In Jesus' Name,
Amen

Journal Entry

_____

_____

_____

_____

_____

_____

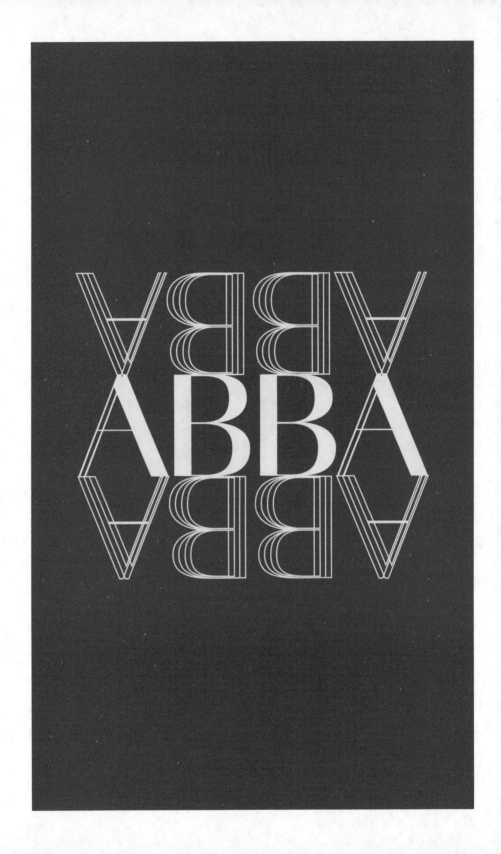

ABBA (Father)

"ABBA" is an Aramaic word for father, used by Jesus and Paul to address God in a relationship of personal intimacy.

"Abba Father" is found three separate times in the Bible: Romans 8:15, Mark 14:36, and Galatians 4:6.

Mark 14:36:
"And He said, 'Abba, Father, all things *are* possible for You. Take this cup away from Me; nevertheless, not what I will, but what You *will*.' "

This is one of the most tender passages in the Bible. For here, we see the struggle within the very heart of Jesus.

In His humanity, death was a choice He would face for our salvation, yet the reality was no one wished to suffer and be beaten and crucified to death.

This was a real cry to Abba, Father for peace and protection.

ABBA

Jesus came to earth of His own free will to die for you and me.

There was no other plan.

Yet when it came down to the very moment in history of His arrest and conviction, Jesus cried out, "Not what I will, but what You will."

Many of us use the name "Father" when we pray. This may be because of our training in the Lord's Prayer. But may I encourage you to include "Abba" with "Father" the next time you pray?

"Abba" is a term used for personal intimacy with God. *My Abba, My Father.*

Prayer is a precious gift of communication where we offer our love, honor, and requests unto God.

Remember the passage we looked at previously?

Matthew 17:21 says, "However, this kind does not go out except by prayer and fasting."

We must use the weapons for warfare given to us by God to battle our enemy.

Prayer and fasting are two of our weapons.

FASTING FOR INTIMACY WITH GOD

Acts 14:23:

"So when they had appointed elders in every church, and prayed with fasting, they commended them to the Lord in whom they had believed."

Paul and Barnabas were preaching the gospel from city to city, and many believed in Jesus as Messiah, but others hated hearing their words and picked up stones to stone Paul to death.

Assuming he was dead, they left him there to die. Paul arose and went into the city with the disciples.

As he gathered the believers together, he commissioned them to continue in the faith and reminded them we all must go through tribulations and trials.

Then they prayed and fasted together before he departed.

Paul was faithful to practice prayer and fasting throughout his ministry.

Even in a passage like this where we see Paul beaten, ridiculed, and left for dead, he still remained faithful.

Paul was the only other person to reference God as "Abba, Father" (Galatians 4:6).

He had a deep understanding of intimacy with God.

1. In our passage today, we read about Jesus in preparing the disciples for His upcoming crucifixion. As He makes His way alone into the garden of Gethsemane, He cries out to Abba, Father, "If it be possible let this cup of death pass from me, but not my will," Jesus prays, "but Your will alone be done." Often, we already know the will of God but end our prayers with "if it be Your will."

What is something you know God wants you to do, but you have struggled moving forward with?

_____

_____

_____

_____

2. Today we spoke about the intimacy of calling on "Abba, Father" in our prayer time.

Take a moment to recite the Lord's Prayer, and make it a little more personal by adding the name "Abba."

Matthew 6:9-13:

"In this manner, therefore, pray: Our (Abba) Father in heaven, hallowed be Your name. Your kingdom come. Your will be done on earth as *it is* in heaven. Give us this day our daily bread. And forgive us our debts, as we forgive our debtors. And do not lead us into temptation but deliver us from the evil one. For Yours is the kingdom and the power and the glory forever. Amen."

3. In Romans 8:15, Paul reminds us, "For you did not receive the spirit of bondage again to fear, but you received the Spirit of adoption by whom we cry out, 'Abba, Father.' "

We do not serve a spirit of fear because we have received a Spirit of Adoption. We have been adopted into the family of Abba, Father. As a child of Abba, we have all our needs met in Christ Jesus. What is something you need to ask God to meet in your life today?

_____

_____

_____

_____

> "

If your day is hemmed in with prayer, it is less likely to come unraveled.

Cynthia Lewis

DEAR ABBA,

Thank You for the intimacy You give me daily.

I love and honor our relationship.

Thank You for being a good, good Father.

You will never leave me or forsake me.

In Jesus' Name,
Amen

Journal Entry

_____

_____

_____

_____

_____

DAILY PRAYER

YESHUA

YESHUA (Savior-Jesus-Messiah)

Jesus, the sweetest name I know. There is just something powerful about the name *Jesus,* maybe because He is our Redeemer, Savior, and Friend.

The name Yeshua, Jesus, means "Savior" ("He will save"). We find this reference in Isaiah 43:3.

Isaiah 43:2-3a:
"When you pass through the waters, I *will be* with you; and through the rivers, they shall not overflow you. When you walk through the fire, you shall not be burned, nor shall the flame scorch you. For I *am* the Lord Your God, The Holy One of Israel, Your Savior..."

How comforting is this verse? Nothing will be able to destroy you because you are the dearly beloved of Yeshua - your Savior.

"Messiah" is another name for Jesus.

"Messiah" literally means "The Anointed King."

The first thing the disciple Andrew did after meeting Jesus was find his brother Simon and tell him, "We have found the Messiah (that is, the Christ)."
John 1:41

The word *Christos* means "The Christ, The Anointed One."

Christ, the Anointed One is equivalent to the Hebrew word "Maschiah," or "Messiah."

Often, we use the name Jesus Christ in speaking of the Lord. We are literally saying, "Savior The Anointed One."

The Gospel of John recounts the disciples' first encounter with Jesus. Their teaching from the Rabbis taught that the Messiah would come and redeem His people. Now, after following John the Baptist and seeing Jesus firsthand, they knew He was here.

John 1:35-40:
"Again, the next day, John stood with two of his disciples. And looking at Jesus as He walked,

he said, 'Behold the Lamb of God!' The two disciples heard him speak, and they followed Jesus. Then Jesus turned, and seeing them following, said to them, 'What do you seek?' They said to Him, 'Rabbi (which is to say, when translated, Teacher), where are You staying?' He said to them, 'Come and see.' They came and saw where He was staying and remained with Him that day (now it was about the tenth hour). One of the two who heard John *speak*, and followed Him, was Andrew, Simon Peter's brother. He first found his own brother Simon, and said to him, **'We have found the Messiah' (which is translated the Christ).** And he brought him to Jesus."

FASTING FOR UNITY

Luke 4:1-4:

"Then Jesus, being filled with the Holy Spirit, returned from the Jordan and was led by the Spirit into the wilderness, being tempted for forty days by the devil. And in those days He ate nothing, and afterward, when they had ended, He was hungry. And the devil said to Him, 'If You are the Son of God, command this stone to become bread.' But Jesus answered him, saying, 'It is written, "Man shall not live by bread alone, but by every word of God." ' "

Did you know Jesus was led by the Spirit to be tempted by the devil? The enemy waits for just the right time to tempt, taunt, and trouble your spirit. But the beautiful part of this scripture is found in verse one. Jesus, being filled with the "Holy Spirit" - that's your defense, your weapon of warfare. Being filled with Holy Spirit.

God has a way of, and reason for,

allowing us to go through temptation. It causes us to depend on His resources and teaches us that Greater is He that is in us than he that is in the world.

First John 4:4: "You are of God, little children, and have overcome them, because He who is in you is greater than he who is in the world."

Jesus knows your struggles and trials firsthand. He can bear witness with our temptations. He is our Mediator, our Go-Between, our Messiah. I believe the reason the Spirit of God led Jesus to be tempted was so we could see firsthand the power of our ability to conquer the enemy. Hebrews teaches us that our High Priest (Jesus) was tempted, yet without sin.

Hebrews 4:15: "For we do not have a High Priest who cannot sympathize with our weaknesses, but was in all *points* tempted as *we are, yet* without sin."

I find so much comfort in our passage today.

Isaiah 43:2-3a:
"When you pass through the waters, I *will* be with you; and through the rivers, they shall not overflow you. When you walk through the fire, you shall not be burned, nor shall the flame scorch you. For I *am* the Lord your God, The Holy One of Israel, your Savior."

1. Is there something you are going through today that you would like to discuss with Jesus? Are there waters or rivers, fires or flames that have you overwhelmed?

Take a moment and talk to Jesus. He is your Savior.

_____

_____

_____

_____

2. Today we highlighted the name of Jesus.
The name given above all names. Our Messiah
and King. Have you experienced the love and
salvation of Jesus? Take a moment and thank
Him for your personal relationship. Write a note
of love to the Lord.

_____

_____

_____

_____

3. Jesus was led by the Spirit to be tempted
by the devil, yet because He was filled with the
Holy Spirit, He could speak back with power and
authority, quoting scripture: "It is written, 'Man
shall not live by bread alone, but by every word
of God.' " Do you have a scripture you like to
quote back to the devil?

Share your favorite Scripture verse here.

_____

_____

_____

_____

A FEW VERSES ABOUT JESUS TO MEDITATE ON TODAY

John 14:6:
"Jesus said to him, 'I am the way, the truth, and the life. No one comes to the Father except through Me.' "

1 Timothy 2:5:
"For *there is* one God and one Mediator between God and men, *the* Man Christ Jesus."

John 3:16:
"For God so loved the world that He gave His only begotten Son, that whoever believes in Him should not perish but have everlasting life."

John 1:1-2:
"In the beginning was the Word, and the Word was with God, and the Word was God. He was in the beginning with God."

John 8:12:
"Then Jesus spoke to them again, saying, 'I am the light of the world. He who follows Me will not walk in darkness, but have the light of life.' "

DEAR JESUS,

You are my Messiah, Lord, and Redeemer.

Thank You for Your sacrifice on Calvary for my salvation.

I confess my sin and shortcomings to You alone and ask for Your forgiveness.

I thank You for Your free gift of salvation. You have saved me!

In Jesus' Name,
Amen

Journal Entry

_____

_____

_____

_____

_____

_____

DAILY PRAYER

HOLY
SPIRIT

HOLY SPIRIT

Holy Spirit

John 14:26

I can't believe we are already here - Day Twenty-One! Today we are going to look at a very special name because it is the name of our Comforter, *Holy Spirit.*

The Holy Spirit is mentioned throughout the whole Bible. But for our reading today, we will look together at John 14:26:

"But the Helper, the Holy Spirit, whom the Father will send in My name, He will teach you all things, and bring to your remembrance all things that I said to you."

Holy Spirit is called the "Helper," "Comforter," "Teacher," and "Guide." God is Trinity. Father, Son, and Spirit. He cannot be divided into three parts. He is all three in one. Much like (but not exactly) I am a wife, a mother, and a daughter. I am not one more than I am the other. Or like an egg, lol... When someone asks you to bring them an egg, you don't say, "Do you want the shell, the yoke, or the whites?" You just bring them an egg. Holy Spirit is and always was. From the beginning. Genesis 1:26: "Let Us make man in Our image. The triune God spoke in unity from the beginning."

- Father-Creator
- Son-Mediator
- Holy Spirit-Comforter

John's Gospel is one of my favorite books in the Bible. It lays out beautifully the plan and pathway of our salvation as well as the power and purpose of the Holy Spirit. Let's look at John 16:5-15.

The Work of the Holy Spirit
John 16:5: "But now I go away to Him who sent Me, and none of you asks Me, 'Where are You going?' But because I have said these things to you, sorrow has filled your heart. Nevertheless I tell you the truth. It is to your advantage that I go away; for if I do not go away, the Helper will not come to you; but if I depart, I will send Him to you. And when He has come, He will convict the world of sin, and of righteousness, and of judgment: of sin, because they do not believe in

Me; of righteousness, because I go to My Father and you see Me no more; of judgment, because the ruler of this world is judged. I still have many things to say to you, but you cannot bear *them* now. However, when He, the Spirit of truth, has come, He will guide you into all truth; for He will not speak on His own *authority*, but whatever He hears He will speak; and He will tell you things to come. He will glorify Me, for He will take of what is Mine and declare *it* to you. All things that the Father has are Mine. Therefore I said that He will take of Mine and declare *it* to you."

When you receive the love and grace of Jesus, you receive the power of His Holy Spirit. The problem is most of us don't know how to release that power into our everyday lives. Let me encourage you to seek out the power and presence of the Holy Spirit. Invite Him to fill you with His power and authority. Holy Spirit is very tender and can be grieved and suppressed. Ephesians 4:30 tells us: "And do not grieve the Holy Spirit of God, by whom you were sealed for the day of redemption." Truthfully, I know when I am walking in the fullness of the Spirit of God and when I am not. When I am not, I simply confess my lack of surrender and ask God to fill me once again with His Power and Spirit.

FILLING OF THE HOLY SPIRIT

Acts 13:2-3:

"As they ministered to the Lord and fasted, the Holy Spirit said, 'Now separate to Me Barnabas and Saul for the work to which I have called them.' Then, having fasted and prayed, and laid hands on them, they sent *them* away."

This passage is an account of the first apostles that were sent out to share the gospel. After Jesus' death, there was a great persecution among the Christians. And yet the power of the early churches grew in number and momentum. The leaders understood that by ministering to the body and fasting together, they could hear and know the will of the Father. The followers of Jesus remembered quite well what had happened in earlier days.

Acts 2:1-2, 14-17 tells us:
"When the Day of Pentecost had fully come, they were all with one accord in

294

one place. And suddenly there came a sound from heaven, as of a rushing mighty wind, and it filled the whole house where they were sitting. But Peter, standing up with the eleven, raised his voice and said to them, 'Men of Judea and all who dwell in Jerusalem, let this be known to you, and heed my words. For these are not drunk, as you suppose, since it is *only* the third hour of the day. But this is what was spoken by the prophet Joel: "And it shall come to pass in the last days, says God, that I will pour out of My Spirit on all flesh; your sons and your daughters shall prophesy, your young men shall see visions, your old men shall dream dreams." ' "

Did you know God wants you to see what He sees? He wants you to have the power and authority to live a life of victory? That is the job of the Holy Spirit. Would you like to be more than a conqueror? The Word of God says it's possible.

Romans 8:37:
"Yet in all these things we are more than conquerors through Him who loved us."

Ask Holy Spirit to breathe His breath of power over you today.

I'm not sure if you made it through each day of our fasting book. If not, let me encourage you to go back and finish the ones you've missed.

I know we get busy, and our schedules are full of "to-do lists," but each name of God is powerful and gives us insight into the character and nature of God.

1. Today we had the opportunity to learn about the power and presence of the Holy Spirit. As we learned, it is easy to suppress the Spirit of God in our lives and become filled with our own agendas and desires. What is one thing you learned about Holy Spirit today?

_____

_____

_____

_____

In Ephesians 4:30, we read that we can grieve the Holy Spirit: "And do not grieve the Holy Spirit of God, by whom you were sealed for the day of redemption."

2. Is there something in your life that might be grieving the Holy Spirit and keeping you from the power and peace of His presence? Talk about it here:

_____

_____

_____

_____

3. We have discussed so many names of God over the last twenty-one days. Each and every one sheds light on a different part of the character and personality of God. If you were to pick one name that stands out as special to you, which one would it be, and why?

Name of God

_____

Why?

_____

_____

_____

_____

_____

> "
>
> Where there is much prayer, there will be much of the Spirit; where there is much of the Spirit, there will be ever-increasing prayer.
>
> Andrew Murray

DEAR HOLY SPIRIT,

Thank You for being my Comforter, Teacher, and Guide.

I pray for Your daily filling and leading in my life. I ask You to place a hedge of protection around me, my family, and my loved ones.

Thank You for giving me power to live each day.

In Jesus' Name,
Amen

Journal Entry

_____

_____

_____

_____

_____

DAILY PRAYER

TEST YOUR KNOWLEDGE

TEST-YOUR-KNOWLEDGE QUIZ

Match the Name of God with His Attribute

1. Elohim	a. Lord My Provider
2. Yahweh / Jehovah	b. The Lord of Hosts
3. El Elyon	c. Comforter
4. Adonai	d. Jealous God
5. El Shaddai	e. God of Salvation
6. El Olam	f. The Lord Is There
7. Jehovah Jireh	g. Lord My Banner
8. Jehovah Rapha	h. God of Knowledge
9. Jehovah Nissi	i. Creator
10. El Qanna	j. Father
11. Jehovah M'Kaddesh	k. The Everlasting God
12. Jehovah Shalom	l. Master
13. Jehovah Sabaoth	m. LORD
14. El Deah	n. Lord My Healer
15. Jehovah Ra'ah	o. The Lord My Shepherd
16. El Moshaah	p. God Almighty
17. Jehovah Tsidkenu	q. Jesus
18. Jehovah Shammah	r. The Lord My Sanctifier
19. Abba	s. The Lord My Peace
20. Yeshua	t. The Lord Our Righteousness
21. Holy Spirit	u. Most High God

ANSWER GUIDE

1-i, 2-m, 3-u, 4-l, 5-p, 6-k, 7-a, 8-n, 9-g, 10-d, 11-r,

12-s, 13-b, 14-h, 15-o, 16-e, 17-t, 18-f, 19-j, 20-q, 21-c

FILL IN THE BLANK

1. Which name of God correlates with the 23rd psalm?

_____

2. Which name of God was in Hannah's prayer?

_____

3. Which name of God was the healing waters of Mara?

_____

4. Which name of God did Moses cry out to as a banner over his enemy?

_____

5. Which name of God appeared at Pentecost?

_____

6. Which name was used for God at creation?

_____

7. Which name of God did Abraham encounter when he offered his son Isaac on the altar?

_____

8. Which name of God means "Self-Existence" (I AM)?

_____

9. Which name means the "Most High God"?

_____

10. Which name means "Lord and Master"?

_____

11. Which name did Abram use when God told him he would be a father to Nations?

_____

12. Which name teaches us not to take the Lord's name in vain?

_____

13. Which name tells us God is a jealous God?

_____

14. Which name tells us we are sanctified?

_____

15. Which name did Gideon call God?

_____

16. Which name refers to God as the "God of Knowledge"?

_____

17. Which name calls God the "God of Salvation"?

_____

18. Which name calls God "Our Righteousness"?

_____

19. Which name of God tells us He is always there?

_____

20. Which name calls God Our Father?

_____

21. Which name tells us He is Messiah?

_____

ANSWER KEY

1. Jehovah Ra'ah

2. Jehovah Sabaoth

3. Jehovah Rapha

4. Jehovah Nissi

5. Holy Spirit

6. Elohim

7. Jehovah Jireh

8. Yahweh

9. El Elyon

10. Adonai

11. El Shaddai

12. El Olam

13. El Qanna

14. Jehovah M'Kaddesh

15. Jehovah Shalom

16. El Deah

17. El Moshaah

18. Jehovah Tsidkenu

19. Jehovah Shammah

20. Abba

21. Jesus

"

The one concern of the devil
is to keep Christians from
praying. He fears nothing from
prayerless studies, prayerless
work, and prayerless religion.
He laughs at our toil, mocks
at our wisdom, but trembles
when we pray.

Samuel Chadwick

RESOURCES

Kay Arthur
Key Principles of Biblical Fasting

Hungrygen.com

Newcreation.org

The Romans Road to Salvation
By Mary Fairchild

APPENDIX

THE ROMANS ROAD TO SALVATION
BY MARY FAIRCHILD

The Romans Road lays out the <u>plan of salvation</u> through a series of Bible verses from the <u>book of Romans</u>. When arranged in order, these verses form an easy, systematic way of explaining the message of salvation.

ROMANS ROAD TO SALVATION
STEP 1 - Everyone needs salvation because all have sinned.
Romans 3:10-12 and 23:
As the Scriptures say, "No one is righteous—not even one. No one is truly wise; no one is seeking God. All have turned away; all have become useless. No one does good, not a single one. ... For everyone has sinned; we all fall short of God's glorious standard." (NLT)

STEP 2 - The price (or consequence) of sin is death.
Romans 6:23:
"For the wages of sin is death, but the free gift of God is eternal life through Christ Jesus our Lord." (NLT)

STEP 3 - <u>Jesus Christ</u> died for our sins. He paid the price for our death.

Romans 5:8:

"But God showed his great love for us by sending Christ to die for us while we were still sinners." (NLT)

STEP 4 - We receive salvation and <u>eternal life</u> through faith in Jesus Christ.

Romans 10:9-10 and 13:

"If you confess with your mouth that Jesus is Lord and believe in your heart that God raised him from the dead, you will be saved. For it is by believing in your heart that you are made right with God, and it is by confessing with your mouth that you are saved.... For "Everyone who calls on the name of the Lord will be saved." (NLT)

STEP 5 - <u>Salvation through Jesus Christ</u> brings us into a relationship of peace with God.

Romans 5:1:

"Therefore, since we have been made right in God's sight by faith, we have peace with God because of what Jesus Christ our Lord has done for us." (NLT)

Romans 8:1:

"So now there is no condemnation for those who belong to <u>Christ Jesus</u>." (NLT)

Romans 8:38-39:

"And I am convinced that nothing can ever separate us from God's love. Neither death nor life, neither angels nor demons, neither our fears for today nor our worries about tomorrow—not even the powers of hell can separate us from God's love. No power in the sky above or in the earth below—indeed, nothing in all creation will ever be able to separate us from the <u>love of God</u> that is revealed in Christ Jesus our Lord." (NLT)

HERE'S HOW TO TAKE YOUR PERSONAL JOURNEY DOWN ROMANS ROAD:

1. Admit you are a sinner.
2. Understand that as a sinner, you deserve death.
3. Believe Jesus Christ died on the cross to save you from sin and death.
4. Repent by turning from your old life of sin to a new life in Christ.
5. Receive, through faith in Jesus Christ, His free gift of salvation.

ADDITIONAL THOUGHTS

_____

_____

_____

_____

_____

_____

_____

_____

_____

_____

_____

_____

_____

_____

_____

_____

_____

Additional Thoughts - Day 12

Additional Thoughts - Day 16

_____

_____

_____

_____

_____

_____

_____

_____

_____

_____

_____

_____

_____

_____

_____

_____

Additional Thoughts - Day 18